THE DENTED FENDER
P R E S E N T S

USING WHAT'S BROKEN TO
Boldly Shine

Barbara R. Lownsbury

www.thedentedfender.com

Using What's Broken to Boldly Shine

© 2018 Barbara Lownsbury

ISBN: 1725780526

Chilidog Press, Loveland, Ohio

For information, contact the author:

Barbara Lownsbury
120 Saint Claire Avenue
Wyoming OH 45215
www.thedentedfender.com

Published by:

Chilidog Press LLC
Loveland, Ohio
www.chilidogpress.com

Cover: Wendy Bentley

MORE PRAISE FOR
USING WHAT'S BROKEN TO BOLDLY SHINE

In writing *Using What's Broken to Boldly Shine*, Barbara Lownsbury has penned a seminal work that combines practical information with God-given wisdom, all very effective in helping others find their way back from life's temporary setbacks. If the art of living is the ability to utilize one's misfortune in a beneficial and constructive fashion, Barbara has provided a superb example of how this is to be accomplished. As an executive coach, I know all too well that we do not always get to choose what happens to us, but we can choose to grow in compassion and wisdom because of those things. The Dented Fender is a compelling and spiritual harvest of redemptive insights that will both excite and challenge the reader.

-Adrian Williams, John Maxwell Leadership Team, Executive Coach, Facilitator, and Speaker

I initially had some reservations about how this book would help, but I gave it a read. I realized that I was "stuck" in my thought/ life processes on some of my internal struggles. What the content was able to convey to me is that God has given freely a "GPS Roadmap" to find my way. Backed by Biblical Scripture references throughout, this book helped me build a solid foundation for my approach on life as well as the people within it. *Using What's Broken to Boldly Shine* is honey to the soul and I <u>HIGHLY</u> recommend it to anyone looking to become "unstuck" and grow in the life that God wants for all of us!

-Dan Baker, a Dented Fender class participant

DEDICATION

To my mom, Karen Wolfe: You are the wind beneath my wings, the shoulders on which I stand. You are a remarkable, talented, loving woman whose openness and caring heart helped mold me into who I am today. This one's for you, Mom. I love you.

To my kids, Wesley, Nick and Ellie: You are my richest blessings and my favorite thing I have ever gotten to do in this life. I am so very proud of each of you! The sacrifices you have made in order to help this project come to life have touched and humbled me. I love you to the moon and beyond...

CONTENTS

CHAPTER 1

THERE IS A WAY OUT
The Tunnel

"Even the longest journey begins where you stand." — Lao-tzu

As I drove around the corner and the view opened up before me, it took my breath away. I was in Death Valley, normally a barren wasteland of desert surrounded by miles of windswept mountains with little vegetation. Yet the valley was alive with color and blooms, coming back to life after higher than average rainfall over the winter. I had come to this desert to see the gorgeous spectacle, but as I pulled over and got out of the car to admire the view, my eye quickly wandered. In the midst of the swaths of purple and yellow and green that covered the mountainside, I couldn't help but notice there were very clear dark spots. Puzzled, I hopped back into my car and drove on for a closer inspection.

Slowly, the dark spots took on the shape of clearly defined rectangles, which eventually materialized into the entrances of old, abandoned mining tunnels. I stopped so I could hike up the mountainside to make a closer inspection. Had some long-gone prospector come out here in search of gold, hoping to find fame and fortune, only to be defeated by the heat and the bleakness of the desert? Had he experienced heartache? Disappointment? My curiosity got the best of me, and before I knew it I found myself carefully working my way past the time-worn wooden planks that warned, "Danger: Do Not Enter," and I wriggled my way in. Probably not one of my brighter moments.

It's an eerie feeling, being in a tunnel. It's a small, enclosed space. When you first enter, you can see the sunlight and the blue sky behind you. There is still a sense of the wind and the world just outside. As you get deeper into the tunnel, however, reality begins to suspend itself. Outside it could be cold, windy, hot or rainy. Once you're deep in a tunnel you don't know any of that. You begin to feel separated, detached. It feels otherworldly.

Walk in deeper still, and light begins to fade until at some point you can barely see it behind you. It's just a little pinprick off in the distance, and even that eventually disappears. You need artificial light just to move forward, or you will be reduced to blindly groping your way through like I was, clinging to the side walls and walking very slowly and carefully. Is there a large hole ahead you might fall into? Or a boulder you might trip over? Is there some huge spider web you might get ensnared in? The truth is that tunnels are dangerous places! A long, dark tunnel is a place that commands respect and attention if you want to make it out safely.

But I found truth in that darkness. Here it is: On our spiritual walks, we all have to go through some pretty dark tunnels. I'm not talking about the short, well-lit tunnels we drive through, honking our horn and laughing with our friends as we go. If only! I'm talking about those long, scary, black tunnels where there is no end in sight, you have no light around you, and there are no friends laughing by your side. You start to feel broken down, abandoned and alone. You wonder where God is inside this stifling, crippling place.

Maybe you're in one of those tunnels right now. There are just so many ways to get stuck in one. It could be a divorce that has you taking shaky steps forward, clinging to the walls and trying desperately to get your bearings. It could be addiction, digging its claws into your arm and dragging you deeper, deeper inside. Maybe it's a financial challenge, an unhealthy relationship, the continued lack of a relationship, or unending, soul sapping loneliness. Maybe you've seen someone you love get stuck in a tunnel, so you followed them inside in an attempt to keep them safe, only to get lost yourself. Even if you feel you've been dragged in against your will, you feel stuck all the same. Sometimes it's just a perfect storm of tangled circumstances that make you wonder why you should even keep trying. Whatever it is, you find your life has been twisted and turned into something else entirely. It can seem overwhelming. Being lost in a tunnel feels hopeless.

Ready for some good news? You don't *have* to stay stuck in that tunnel. In fact, you don't have to stay stuck at all. God has a plan for you. His plan is to prosper you, not to harm you. He wants to give you back hope and a real future (Jeremiah 29:11). He wants to heal you and make you whole again, to cleanse you from the filth and fill you with purity and joy. In Ezekiel 36:26 He says, "I will give you a new heart and put a new spirit in you; I will remove from you your heart of stone and give you a heart of flesh." And that's just a taste of what He has in store for you.

If you're like me, your first thought might be, "Yeah, right. That sounds *way* too good to be true. If you really *knew* what [insert current issue] was like, you couldn't say that."

That's why I'm here. You see, I *can* say that, and I can say it with conviction. This isn't a theory or mere religious platitudes for me, or some sort of God Band-Aid I'm trying to put on a gaping wound. The lessons I will share are wrought from deeply challenging, emotionally crippling trials I have gone through myself. I have been through tunnels so dark and deep I could taste the fear in my mouth and feel the cloying air of despair choking my lungs, where even my ability to remember that the tunnel had an end seemed to vanish.

I will share with you pieces of my journey, the key pieces. The ones that really mattered, that ended up becoming those huge life lessons that not only pull you out of that tunnel, but into a sun-filled life that can be so wonderful, so freeing, it's hard to put into words.

My number one lesson? God is such an amazing God! He specializes in bringing light into dark places. No problem, no challenge is too tough for Him—not even yours. When you feel crushed and alone, paralyzed and unable to move, He meets you where you are and gently, lovingly takes your hand to help you stand up again. He will provide enough light for you to take each step forward, one at a time, until you finally make it through. There's a reason, after all, He is called the light of the world.

Does this mean I never struggle, that my life is perfect and happy all the time? No. I still have challenging days and seasons where I can begin to feel that sense of despair and desperation again, and the tunnel beckons. The difference now is that God has taught me how to keep from getting sucked in, how to fight back, and how to keep winning the overall war even if sometimes I lose an individual battle.

The lessons and principles I will share with you can be your guide to find your own personal exit from the darkness. Just as your individual challenges are unique, so will be your journey. Yet these guiding principles, like God, are universal and they can propel you forward if you grab hold of them.

Remember, too, guides don't work the same as a map. They take into account the emotional scenery, the pace at which you need to move, the nuances of what is going on around you. While they won't necessarily move you from Point A to Point B immediately, you will learn how to move forward in your journey, and to no longer let the dents and bruises of life define you. More important, you will begin the process of healing wholeheartedly and being renewed.

These principles and the lessons contained within will be discussed at length in the chapters that follow, but for now here is a brief summary:

LIFE-GUIDING PRINCIPLES

1. *VISION*: Begin to believe you can heal and change because God can heal and change you.
2. *CONNECTION*: Learn to tie into God and to others who are on your side and want to help you heal.

3. *BRAVERY*: Start to push past your fear and learn from your challenges.

4. *INTENTIONALITY*: Establish concrete, specific steps to change your situation.

5. *CONSISTENCY*: Train for the important step of developing and maintaining healthy habits.

6. *BOLDLY SHINE*: Step back and watch what God can do, marking the moments of victory and learning to refine your vision as you listen for God's ongoing direction for your life.

If only just reading that list could give you instant transformation. Sorry—it won't. Even reading this book and memorizing each step won't do it for you. But if you begin to put these principles into practice, if you begin to lift your eyes and reach out to God in these areas, you will begin to heal and move forward. Truly.

It's important to remember that this process isn't linear. In other words, you won't start off with VISION, get one in place, and then—bam!—you've got that down so you can move on to CONNECTION. Rather, think of each step as being interconnected, woven together by the Holy Spirit over time—sort of like cogs that only work when they are turning together. It is a constant process that will carry you forward throughout life. One month you may experience some tremendous growth in your personal BRAVERY but struggle more with INTENTIONALITY. Some days you will mark a BOLDLY SHINING moment only to feel challenged to maintain your CONSISTENCY the very next day. Not only is that okay, it's normal.

But I encourage you to read each of the principles in order. Each quality builds on the one that comes before it; each will progress forward from the previous step. It's sort of like playing tennis. You have to know how to hold a racquet before you can start hitting the ball. You have to know how to hit the ball before you start attempting to play against someone. Yet even as you advance in your skills at tennis, you should routinely come back to check on how you're gripping your racquet, if you're hitting the ball correctly and so forth. That's how growth works.

Know upfront this guide isn't intended to "fix" you, or to tell you that if you simply do steps 1 through 5 you'll be happy. I'll tell you right now I don't have all the answers, and the truth is I don't trust people who claim they do. Instead, my goal is to help you find your own answers, and to wade through what that process might look like for you, using key principles to guide you along your way. It may not be as easy, but I can tell you this—it is always more empowering in the end. There will be lots of pragmatics I will share along the way, but each person's journey will be different depending on where that person is on the path.

Bottom line: God *wants* to help you where you are *right now*. He's not looking at where you should be or thinking about what a failure you are to have gotten stuck in that tunnel in the first place. He's not sitting around waiting to criticize your wrong decisions or chastise you for getting stuck. All He's asking is for you to allow Him to show up. You don't even have to take a step toward Him yet. Just look up and notice He's next to you—and He will begin to do the rest.

You see, at this point in my life I definitely know I am a hopeless sinner, but I've also learned that God is incredibly greater than my sin, and in fact sees me through a completely different lens. Sin isn't what gets me into "trouble" with God; sin merely gets in the way of me seeing His hand in those dark places, of hearing his loving voice in those places of crushing anguish. Yes, it can often create those places of anguish, too, but that is why God doesn't like sin. He absolutely hates to see me hurting.

And God hates to see you hurting, too. He looks at your heart, crushed and battered like a bird with a broken wing, and wants to heal and make you whole again. He wants to make you soar. He won't always do it in the way you expect, or in the timing you want. But He will do it for you. God has a remarkable history of taking the broken things, the shamed things of this world and making them the shining jewels in His crown.

You are that jewel.

Sit tight, dig in, and let's begin this journey together. Let God guide you back out of that tunnel into the light. It will be a journey of self-discovery, of growth, of challenge and of healing. It won't be linear. It won't be easy. The one thing I can guarantee, though, is that it will be worthwhile. *You* are worthwhile. God has so many dreams for you—even when you don't believe it.

SUMMARY

On our spiritual journey, we sometimes get stuck in some dark, challenging tunnels. Fortunately, God can take us through those tunnels in a way that makes us better for the process. He specializes in bringing light into dark places, removing from us the hurt and the bitterness, and instead replacing it with joy and peace. Remember, this book isn't designed to "fix" you. Rather, you will be given principles and practical steps that will help you move forward on your spiritual journey and toward the tunnel exit.

There are 6 life-guiding principles:
1. VISION
2. CONNECTION
3. BRAVERY
4. INTENTIONALITY
5. CONSISTENCY
6. BOLDLY SHINE

These principles all work together to lead you toward transformation and renewal, a life that boldly shines.

FOR FURTHER THOUGHT

In response to chapter one:
1. What is something you heard about God?
2. What is something you'd like to receive?
3. What is something you heard about yourself?
4. What do you hope to get out of this book?
5. Do something this week that emotionally fills you.

CHAPTER 2

DISCOVER THE EXIT
Vision

"If the doors of perception were cleansed, everything would appear to man as it is—infinite." — William Blake

All of us, at some point, start off with a vision for ourselves. It is rare to come across a 5-year-old who doesn't have a vision of whom he or she will become. They're not afraid to dream big. Astronaut? You bet. Ballerina? Of course. President of the United States? I could do it if I really wanted to.

None of us start off in life saying, "I want to be a failure," or, "I want to grow up and get divorced someday," or, "Someday when I'm older I hope I'll become a drug addict, or a widow, or sleep around with lots of men, or fail at business and go bankrupt." Those things just don't cross a kid's personal radar. Even if they see those things around them--drugs, promiscuity, divorce, etc. –they're convinced they're going to be different. It's one of those things we love about kids. They're full of hope. They don't think about the odds. They simply have faith.

Life has a way of showing up and kicking the tar out of that simple, child-like faith, doesn't it? By the time most of us have a few decades under our belt, our views are very, very different. It doesn't take much time to do an internet search and learn that your average 20-something no longer believes in the sanctity of marriage or the stereotypical American dream of "find a job, get married, be successful, etc." They are too cynical because of all they have seen. And the truth is, as a nation we are much more cynical about life and our possibilities in general.[1]

Why? How did this happen? It's a long, long list. It can be from our own choices and decisions, or from others' choices and decisions. Ultimately, the impact is the same. We begin to let our circumstances, our weaknesses, other people, even our religion define who we can or cannot be, versus trusting our inner compass—the Holy Spirit—to guide us on the path that is destined for us. God wants us to have vision for our life. He wants us to believe in possibilities, even after our own vision for our life has been crushed. Maybe even *especially* then.

Now, if you're the skeptical type, as I can be, you might sit back in your chair right now and think, "Really? Vision?! Look, I'm just trying to make it through this hour faking that I'm a functioning, rational adult. I don't have time for vision."

I'm here to tell you the exact opposite is true. You can't afford *not* to create a God-given vision for what your life can be. In Proverbs 29:18, Solomon tells us, "Where there is no vision, the people perish." Wow. That's a pretty big statement. He's essentially telling us if we don't have vision for our lives, we're going to die. It's not necessarily a physical death he's talking about here, either, but an emotional death of the heart and soul. It's part of why we feel so lost in our lives. We've forgotten how to have vision for ourselves.

"Fine," you may say. "I need vision. I have no idea how I'm supposed to get vision when my life is lying in tatters all around me, and I feel like an emotional train wreck most days."

Remember when I talked about God showing up right where you are? How you don't even need to take a step toward Him yet, just simply look-up and acknowledge He's there? That's actually how vision starts—by opening yourself up to begin looking for vision. It's amazing how it will start to show up in the most unexpected ways and find you. We will delve into how to connect—or reconnect—with God extensively in the next chapter, but for now, just begin to simply lift your head up and look for ways God may be directing you.

VISION & PURPOSE

The next step is to begin to realize that literally everything we go through, when we put it in the context of our walk with God, has a purpose. God doesn't want us to have miserable lives. Quite the opposite. In fact, in John 10:10 Jesus says, "I came to give life with joy and abundance." But God, because He loves us, can use the tragedies, the hurts, the ugly moments in our lives to achieve something greater, something infinitely beautiful from the ashes of the devastation around us. Let's unpack this.

When Michelangelo, arguably the greatest sculpture in the history of mankind, began the work of creating his next marble masterpieces, he didn't see what you and I see. Where we would look and find nothing more than a rough-hewn block of marble, he would see the exact creation he intended to make staring out at him, waiting to be released by each masterful stroke of his hammer and chisel.

To God, you are His masterpiece. When you get up and look in the mirror each morning, you see your wrinkles, your flaws, your imperfections. You see the rough-hewn marble. But God, in His masterful wisdom, sees you as the absolutely beautiful and perfect masterpiece that you are within. He knows exactly who you are meant to be.

The Bible puts it this way (2 Corinthians 3:18): "Now all of us reflect the glory of the Lord as if we are mirrors; and so we are being transformed, metamorphosed, into His very *own* image in ever increasing splendor and from one degree of glory to another, just as the Spirit of the Lord accomplishes it." With each challenge, with each situation, with every tear that is shed, joy that is felt, and victory that is achieved, God is transforming you into this beautiful, amazing, exquisite thing that is awesome to behold.

Unfortunately, it doesn't always feel that way. In the midst of the hammering and chiseling, we can feel pain. Some of the cuts are tiny and small, requiring delicate, precise work. Sometimes large chunks need to be taken away so major portions of our character can be hammered out. These deep times of refining are where we can feel the most pain, the most lost, the most insecure.

And it's important to note that not all large blows and cuts come from the Lord. Sometimes the enemy sneaks in and tries to chisel off pieces in a hurtful, careless way and we have no control over it. We can also get so wrapped up in our own personal hell and fear that when we see a hammer coming, even if we know it's from God, we reach up and try to swipe it away, causing the hammer to strike the wrong spot and doing great damage to us in the process.

I had the privilege of visiting the Accademia Gallery in Florence, Italy that houses the amazing sculpture of *David*, carved by the great Michelangelo himself. As you enter the gallery, you're ushered into a long, narrow hall. At the end of the hallway stands the *David* in all its miraculous glory. But all along the path leading up to him you see partially carved blocks of stone. Fascinatingly enough, these were all of Michelangelo's mistakes. Some had very little carving; some were almost completely formed, like a body that had somehow been trapped in stone. While several of these pieces were practice stones, some were works of art in progress destroyed by one wrong cut. They are called *The Lost Souls*.

Sometimes we feel like that, don't we? Like that last big cut in our life has ruined us and destroyed us in a way from which we can never fully recover. The pain is too great; the wound is too deep. We feel trapped, unable to be released from the stony prison of our minds and hearts.

I'm so glad God is my sculpture, not Michelangelo! You see, God doesn't make mistakes. He doesn't use some of us for practice marble. He is the Master Sculptor, the great I Am. When the thief comes in to deface and destroy us, God knows how to work around that bad cut and *still* release the masterpiece that is you. Even if you've been the one knocking that hammer to all the wrong places, wounding and scarring and destroying yourself until all you see left is a pile of rubble, God is still God. If you'll let Him, He still knows how to pick up each tiny piece and recreate it into something even better, something miraculous.

The Old Testament prophet Isaiah put it this way (Isaiah 61:1-3): "[God] has sent me to repair broken hearts, to proclaim freedom for the captives and release from darkness for the prisoners ... to give them a beautiful crown instead of ashes, to anoint them with gladness instead of sorrow, to wrap them in victory, joy and praise instead of depression and sadness. People will call them magnificent…"

You may still be sitting back, arms crossed, thinking that I just don't get it, that I don't understand. And to some degree you're right. I don't completely or deeply understand your personal challenge. Even if I had many, many free hours to hear your story, I would never fully understand *exactly* what you feel. After all, Proverbs 14:10 tells us, "Only the person involved can know his own bitterness or joy—no one else can really share it."

Guess what? God does. He absolutely, positively "gets" it in all of its ugly, messy, painful glory. He understands it even more deeply and even more clearly than you do. He knows without even one bit of hesitation how to heal you and empower you to move forward. He has the advantage of not only seeing you where you are right now, at this very moment, far more clearly than you do, but can also see the amazing person He intends for you to become.

So, lean on His vision for you until you begin to believe what He has in store. Read the scriptures on how God feels about you over and over and over again until they begin to feel more real, until they begin to seep into your soul. Write them on index cards and carry them with you if that helps. I've put some of my favorites at the end of this chapter to give you a starting point.

WHEN VISION IS CRUSHED

How do I know all this? How have I come to believe it's even possible? I wish I could say it all came from researching others' stories, about how others have overcome tremendous obstacles through faith—and certainly I have done that. But the deepest lessons I've learned have come from watching my own dreams get shoved into a wine press and crushed into oblivion, only to emerge better and stronger, new and precious.

My biggest dream, bar none, was to have a successful marriage that lasted until death do us part. I wanted that for myself; I wanted that for my children; I wanted to be that witness for God. I tried to arrange my life in such a way as to guarantee that outcome. Though I went into the full-time ministry as a young woman because I felt called by God to do so, I also deeply believed that if I married a man who had that same passion and vision, that same desire to please God, we could weather any storm.

Within the first month of my married life, I began to realize that achieving the goal of a great marriage was going to be incredibly challenging, and not in the "he squeezes the toothpaste the wrong way" sense. It was in a fundamental, deep-rooted way that sent chills down my spine. I had moments of desolation and despair, feeling trapped in years of drudgery, trying to make things work. How had my plan failed so miserably? Still, I had faith that God was even stronger than the challenges in front of me and I regained my faith, vision, and hope relatively quickly.

Nearly twenty years and three children later, I can honestly say we had more good years than bad; God helped us overcome much. But I also learned that while it takes two to get married, it really only takes one to get a divorce. And no matter how badly you may want to work on things personally, there's no way to make someone else have that same determination and conviction. Most importantly, I learned you can't continue to give away virtually every piece of who you are to appease someone else's vision of who they want you to be. It's almost surreal to write each of these concepts in brief sentences when in reality it took me large chunks of time to wrestle with and accept each of these statements, not just intellectually, but on a deep emotional level—to the point where they became the freeing truths from God they were meant to be.

As hard as it was to see my marriage fail—and I mark having to tell my children as one of the darkest, most challenging moments of my life—I still clung to the belief I could at least offer them a good example of how divorced parents could be. I wanted to give them the smoothest transition humanly possible. Even though we failed each other, we could still get along and put aside our differences for their benefit.

When even that dream was crushed, I cried out to God many times asking the eternal "Why?!" The ugliness that ensued, punctuated by bankruptcy and home foreclosure and all that those entail (How will I even be able to get groceries to feed my kids this week? How can I afford gas to be able to work? Etc.), took me to the absolute brink emotionally.

Your story may be similar to mine, or it may be very different. Your challenges may come from outside forces or from within. Yet whatever the circumstances, that sense of desperation and despair washing over you is not the end of your story. It hasn't been the end of mine.

Perhaps like me you've heard God never gives you more than you can handle. The truth is we do get more than we can handle, more than God ever wanted us to have to handle in the first place. Thankfully, He doesn't expect us to handle it. I've learned I don't have to reach inside and pull out superhuman strength. And neither do you. Why? Because God *is* your strength. He's the one who can lift you up. What you're grappling with is far more than you can handle, but it's not too much for God. Paul writes in 2 Corinthians 1:8:

> *We don't want you in the dark, friends, about how hard it was when all this came down on us in Asia province. It was so bad we didn't think we were going to make it. We felt like we'd been sent to death row, that it was all over for us. As it turned out, it was the best thing that could have happened. Instead of trusting in our own strength or wits to get out of it, we were forced to trust God totally—not a bad idea since he's the God who raises the dead! And he did it, rescued us from certain doom. And he'll do it again, rescuing us as many times as we need rescuing.*

Paul knew what it meant to struggle to the point of facing death, only to see God show up and rescue him physically, emotionally and spiritually. Born from such experience was the belief that God would be able to rescue him again and again. Paul regained his vision for what God could do in the worst of circumstances.

God is a good God. He's not out to tempt you, to ruin or destroy you. Yet we also live in a fallen, broken world, which means challenges are going to come our way that are far greater than we can handle on our own. When you and I learn to lean into God during these storms, He rescues us in ways we could never anticipate or imagine.

Now I'm no apostle. I'm not some spiritual guru with supernatural skills. If only! Amazingly, though, when I began to cry out to God, He began to answer—quietly at first, but more loudly as I began to trust in the vision He was laying out for me of a life free from financial worry, emotional pain, and a crippled heart. My old dreams were replaced with new, remarkable ones that inspired me to want to move forward.

As I began to regain vision for my life, my connection with God grew stronger. He replaced my fear with a greater sense of bravery, allowing me to learn from my situation instead of being dominated by it. I became very intentional in how I approached my challenges. Solutions started to become clear. I grew in my ability to consistently move forward to boldly shine. Yet it all started with vision.

THOUGHTS, ACTIONS & VISION

What you will find is when your thoughts and beliefs change, your actions follow. If you remain stuck inside your tunnel, refusing to look up and move, you will remain as you are—stuck, hopeless, and helpless. But if you begin to look up, to see God's hand reaching for you, to begin a dialogue with Him, and ultimately to reach out toward His hand so he can start to lead you to a safe place, you will find your feet begin to move. You begin the process of moving forward again because you know He is leading you to a better place—the place He showed you. You're moving toward your vision.

James 5:10-11 reads, "The prophets who declared the word of the Lord are your role models, my brothers and sisters, for what it means to live patiently in the face of suffering. Look, we count as blessed those who persevered under hardship." I used to hate these types of scriptures. How could it possibly be a blessing to have to be patient in suffering? I wanted the blessing part; I just didn't want the trial and suffering.

Now I understand. It's because these Christ followers knew the richness and breadth of the blessings that would come from such experiences. They knew in the depths of challenge and despair that you and I would also see the depth of God's mercy and love in ways we had only glimpsed before. Our faith becomes bedrock, unshakeable. Even though our knees may still quiver and tremble and doubt can shadow our hearts, His light pierces through more quickly each time we learn to trust and surrender to His voice, His vision for each of us.

Listen to the vision James lays out for us in James 1:2-4: "Consider it pure joy, my brothers and sisters, whenever you face trials of many kinds, because you know that the testing of your faith produces perseverance. Let perseverance finish its work so that you may be mature and complete, *not lacking anything*" (emphasis added). Now that's a great vision!

Beginning to regain a God-given vision for your life is an important start. Think of movies like *Rocky, Glory, Gladiator, The Patriot*, and *Rudy*. Why do we find these stories so inspiring? The truth is we all like to root for the underdog. There's something about seeing someone overcome incredible obstacles and come out on top that resonates deeply within each of us. In this fallen, broken world, each of us knows life is rarely fair, easy or just. Seeing someone not only survive but actually thrive after such challenges inspires us to move forward.

God wants *you* to be His personal inspiration story. He wants to take *your* situation and use it to not only create all of these amazing victories in your own life, but to hold it up as a beacon of light to the people around you as well. When you feel down, discouraged and defeated, reach out to God and fight to maintain His vision for you. Remember that when God sees you, He doesn't see the crumbling pieces of the person you used to be. He sees the masterpiece you are becoming. That hope is what you're reaching toward.

Alexander Graham Bell put it this way: "When one door closes another door opens, but we so often look so long and so regretfully upon the closed door that we do not see the ones which open for us." You can't change what has happened any more than I can. I will always be someone who went through a divorce, bankruptcy and foreclosure. Yet those events don't define me. They merely served as conduits to turn me toward a better, richer path I might not have found otherwise.

The lessons I would learn from the fires of hardship are the richest, most remarkable lessons I have learned in life so far. Of course, I would have loved to learn them differently, but I wouldn't trade what I've gained on the inside for anything. Why? Because the peace and surrender I experience regularly now are priceless. My joy has been restored. My confidence in my value before God is deep. It's this wholeness, this greater, deeper, richer level of living that God wants for you, too.

What will your vision be? Will it be a drug free life? Will it be a season of growth, joy and healing? Perhaps it's to get a different job or a different career, or to redefine your life now that your career has ended. Maybe it's to become financially independent, or to begin to connect with the larger world around you. It could be simply to feel alive again. Sometimes it's finding the next step, and then the next, and then the next again and again and again. That's it! There's no bigger vision, no grand picture—just the next step.

Whatever the vision God lays before you, begin to imagine what your life could be like if this was your truth. Take time to actually picture it. Grab hold of His vision for you, big or small, and begin to make it your own.

SUMMARY

Vision is crucial. Begin to look to God and ask Him to show you His vision for you. As you do, realize that what you go through has value and worth when you put it into God's hands. No matter what it is, He can find a way to use if for good if you let Him.

Vision is also part of how you will begin to access God's strength in your life. As your vision begins to change to God's vision for you, your actions will naturally begin to follow.

FOR FURTHER THOUGHT

1. Take time out in each day to ask God to give you a new vision for what your life can be.

2.   Don't be afraid to dream about what your life would look like if your challenge was healed or removed. Write down or draw what a changed life would look like for you on a day-to-day basis.

3.   Write down or memorize scriptures that you personally connect with. Write them on your bathroom mirror so you see them each morning, or put a few on your refrigerator so you see them throughout the day. Place them on index cards and carry them with you so you can pull them out when you're feeling emotionally challenged or drained. Remind yourself often of God's vision of who you are.

4.   If you run across quotes or sayings you love which fit into your God-given vision, post or memorize those as well.

MY FAVORITE SCRIPTURES

This is by no means an exhaustive list, but below are some of the scriptures I have posted around my home and office to help me hold on to my vision. If you're not sure how to find scriptures for yourself, I've included some quick tips at the end to help you.

The Lord your God is with you, He is mighty to save. He will take great delight in you, He will quiet you with his love, He will rejoice over you with singing. — Zephaniah 3:17

I'm absolutely convinced that nothing—nothing living or dead, angelic or demonic, today or tomorrow, high or low, thinkable or unthinkable—absolutely nothing can get between us and God's love because of the way that Jesus our Master has embraced us. — Romans 8:38-39.

For as high as the heavens are above the earth, so great is his love for those who love him; as far as the east is from the west, so far has he removed our sins from us. — Psalm 103:11-12

He is close to the broken hearted and saves those who are crushed in spirit. — Psalm 34:18

Do you not know? Have you not heard? The Lord is the everlasting God, the Creator of the ends of the earth. He will not grow tired or weary, and His understanding no one can fathom. He gives strength to the weary and increases the power of the weak. Even youths grow tired and weary, and young men stumble and fall; but those who hope in the Lord will renew their strength. They will soar on wings like eagles; they will run and not grow weary, they will walk and not be faint. — Isaiah 40:28-31

"For I know the plans I have for you," declares the Lord. "Plans to prosper you

and not to harm you. Plans to give you a hope and a future." — Jeremiah 29:11

I am with you always, to the very end. — Matthew 28:20

See, I have you engraved on the palms of my hands. — Isaiah 49:16

This is how we know that we belong to the truth and how we set our hearts at rest in his presence: if our hearts condemn us, we know that God is greater than our hearts, and he knows everything. — 1 John 3:19-20

And may you have the power to understand, as all God's people should, how wide, how long, how high, and how deep his love is. — Ephesians 3:18

Do not put your trust in princes, in human beings, who cannot save. When their spirit departs, they return to the ground; on that very day their plans come to nothing. Blessed are those whose hope is in the Lord their God. He is the Maker of heaven and earth, the sea, and everything in them—he remains faithful forever. — Psalm 146:3-6

I have told you these things so that in me you may have peace. In this world you will have trouble. But take heart! I have overcome the world. — John 16:33

Finding Scriptures: At the back of many Bibles is something called a Concordance, which is just a fancy name for an alphabetized index of words. You can look up words like "unfailing" or "love" or "precious" and you will find scriptures containing that word. Some Bibles have a topical index, which gives you topics such as "love" and then lists key scriptures that teach about it. Both concordances and topical indexes can be bought as separate books. You can also check them out from your local library or go online to biblestudytools.com/concordances or biblegateway.com/topical. Bible Gateway also has about every version of the Bible you can think of, available to explore for free online.

Another great way to find scriptures is to read books of the Bible that focus on the topic you want to learn about. Some Bibles will give a brief summary of the main lessons from each book right before the first chapter. Others will give you a list at the back of the Bible. Both of the websites above will give you lessons as well. Some great books for gaining vision are Joshua, Nehemiah, Mark, Romans, Ephesians, and 1 John. Both Psalms and Proverbs are also full of nuggets of wisdom and contain many verses about God's love and vision for you. Don't have a Bible? Most churches will give you one for free. You can also order a free Bible from biblesforamerica.org. Happy hunting!

REFERENCES

[1]Rosen, J. (1995, Nov-Dec). *Cynicism and the Faltering Public Will. The IRE Journal.* Retrieved from http://www.pbs.org/wgbh/pages/frontline/shows/press/other/rosen.html

CHAPTER 3

MEET YOUR GUIDE
Connection

"Sometimes, reaching out and taking someone's hand is the beginning of a journey. At other times, it is allowing another to take yours." — Vera Nazarian

When you're hurting, it is so *hard* to remember God.

When I was a little girl my father took me to an airport to watch the planes land. He was fascinated by planes and took a moment to share that passion with me. We stood together on an old wooden flight observation deck. I don't quite remember how it happened, but I somehow got a large splinter lodged in my finger that went in quite deep. I'd never had a splinter before so I was terrified. It took my dad quite a bit of coaxing to get me to even let him look at it. He kept his promise to me to not pull it out, but instead took me home so my mother could tend to it.

What happened next is still burned in my brain all these years later because it felt so traumatic to a young 3-year-old girl. My parents cornered me in the bathroom, my mother with tweezers in hand. They promised, as most parents do, that it wouldn't hurt. I hesitantly held out my finger, cautiously hopeful, only to get sucker punched by the pain as cold, metal tweezers dug into the soft flesh of my finger pad to do their work. Big tears sprang forth as I screamed out in shock. That cautious hopefulness was quickly replaced by an overwhelming sense of betrayal and hurt.

Hot on the heels of removing the splinter, my mom insisted on putting some Mercurochrome on the wound to prevent infection. Now maybe you've never had the lovely experience of having Mercurochrome put on an open wound, but let me tell you—even as an adult you would say it stings like crazy. Once again, my parents promised me it wouldn't hurt. Naturally, I didn't believe them.

My dad gently took me by the shoulders, looked me in the eye, and promised me it wouldn't be bad. Full of fear, I reluctantly held out my finger. As my mom dabbed on the dreaded medicine, I screamed as only a 3-year-old could, completely unprepared for how painful it would feel. For my outburst I was scolded, which felt like adding insult to injury.

Now I realize my parents were doing the very best they knew how with a terrified and irrational 3-year old. Yet to this day I can't look at Mercurochrome without a small internal shudder. And while my parents learned from that point forward to be honest about what something might feel like, my trust level with them took a serious nose-dive that day, and it took time to rebuild.

When we're hurt, deeply hurt, we can feel a lot like that small child—bewildered and in pain, shocked and unsure of what to do. We want to turn to someone for help, but they've let us down before, so it's hard to trust them. And sometimes, we feel that way toward God.

Unlike a small child, we have developed some pretty intricate defense mechanisms over the years to protect ourselves from pain and betrayal. We become stoic or paste on our best smile and act like it doesn't really hurt, even though anyone else can see it obviously does. Or we refuse to discuss it at all, effectively locking everyone out so we can sit alone in our pain. We may seek to numb it with alcohol, drugs, sex, food, internet surfing, porn or excessive work and activity. Or we may run around and cry wildly to anyone who will listen, yet never really stop to hear the answer or be sure the person we're sharing with has any idea how to help. But the fact remains that we still have a wound that needs to be addressed and healed, and we can't truly move forward until we acknowledge it.

PLUG INTO YOUR POWER SOURCE

There is a better way to go about healing than hiding behind our defensive posturing. We know that doesn't really change anything anyway. The key to healing, as simple as it may seem, is to genuinely connect with God. He is your power source, your link to unlimited strength and hope. He is your guide, your North Star. He takes away your emotional punishment and replaces it with peace and joy. Just as we must plug something into a power source in order for it to work, we must learn to plug into this power source in order for us to work the way God intended. We must learn to connect with God in a deeper, more personal way.

Too often we view God as some sort of universal candy man, granting wishes and dreams to the good little boys and girls of the world. If we're really, really good we might get something. If we're really, really bad we don't even bother going to the candy man. He'll just say no. So, we try to steal it any way we can. Or we can be like a child who felt like they deserved a piece of candy, by golly. We walk up with our long list of all we've done right and feel robbed when we don't get what we think we deserve. These views don't represent God. It's not how He thinks. Thankfully, it's not how He works.

God wants a genuine relationship with you, one you're actively engaged in. Think about the best primary relationships you've had in your life. It could be a husband or wife, girlfriend or boyfriend, a parent or sibling, or a very close friend. These are the people you *want* to spend time with. You think about them often. You make decisions around them. You miss them when you don't see them. You trust them and can confide in them. You know they can handle your problems without judgment or freaking out. They've got your back, and you've got theirs. In other words, you are actively engaged in living life with this person. Yet if either of you stops actively engaging, you drift apart and sometimes out of each other's lives altogether. Your relationship with God works much the same way (though you would be the one drifting away—God never will).

Connection starts first and foremost by realizing God wants to engage with you in a way that's meaningful and real. Think about it. As people, we want to be loved for who we are, not for what we do, though certainly what we do is an expression of who we are. But no one wants it to be said, "Well, I love Dan because he's rich," or, "I love Sharon because she's pretty." We want them to love and respect us for the qualities that make up *who* we are, quirks and all.

Why are we this way? I believe it's because we are made in His image (Genesis 1:27). We intuitively look for the same things in others that God looks for with us. We are wired to want something genuine in our lives because it's a reflection of what God wants to share with us. And that's what God wants to share with you. God wants a genuine relationship with you. Not one that's based on religious ritual, or guilt, or duty, or so you can see what you can get—but because you genuinely love God the way He loves you.

The challenge becomes: How do we engage in relationship with God in a way that's meaningful? How do we begin to trust Him in the midst of such deep challenge and pain? I've learned it starts by realizing how much He loves and cares about us. Again, consider the following scriptures:

> *I am with you always, to the very end.* — Matthew 28:20
> *The Lord your God is with you, He is mighty to save. He will take great delight in you, He will quiet you with his love, He will rejoice over you with singing.* — Zephaniah 3:17
>
> *I'm absolutely convinced that nothing—nothing living or dead, angelic or demonic, today or tomorrow, high or low, thinkable or unthinkable—absolutely nothing can get between us and God's love because of the way that Jesus our Master has embraced us.* — Romans 8:38-39
>
> *Do you not know? Have you not heard? The Lord is the everlasting God,*

the Creator of the ends of the earth. He will not grow tired or weary, and His understanding no one can fathom. He gives strength to the weary and increases the power of the weak. Even youths grow tired and weary, and young men stumble and fall; but those who hope in the Lord will renew their strength. They will soar on wings like eagles; they will run and not grow weary, they will walk and not be faint. — Isaiah 40:28-31

See, I have you engraved on the palms of my hands. — Isaiah 49:16

The first step is to simply look up, away from yourself, and see God's outstretched arm. Just see Him standing right there in the midst of your maelstrom of emotion, waiting to help pull you up and out of the misery you're sitting in. You no longer have to hide because His arm leads to healing and emotional health, to strength after strength to carry you through your journey.

GET REAL

Once you realize He's there, the next step is to start getting real. God loves it when we're genuine with Him. Yet too often we're afraid to be real, painfully real, before our Creator. We tend to sugarcoat things because we know we're standing before the Maker of the Universe, the Great I Am. For me, sometimes I am so busy knowing what I should be thinking, about what's right and wrong about my thinking, that I forget to take the time to discover what it is I actually feel—and get it out before God. I get caught up in the "good little girl" syndrome again.

In fact, being "good" and being "happy" and "positive" can actually be counter-productive during times of trial. When you're so busy convincing yourself you're okay while masking the silent fear that you're not, your heart gets lost in the process. Connecting with God requires you to put the mask down and force yourself to step into what's really going on within.

The truth is, God knows exactly what you're feeling anyway. If you're angry with Him, He already knows it. If you're feeling disappointed with Him, or selfish, lustful, depressed, bitter or hateful, He knows. Hebrews 4:13 says, "No creature can hide from God: God sees all. Everyone and everything is exposed, opened for His inspection; and He's the One we will have to explain ourselves to." He's not afraid of your anger, your curses, or anything else you can throw at Him.

Yet know this as well: There's something about getting out our true hearts before God that is freeing. Psalm 62:7-8 says, "My salvation and my honor depend on God; he is my mighty rock, my refuge. Trust in him at all times, you people; pour out your hearts to him, for God is our refuge." When we learn to get real with God, to no longer be afraid to be messy, He becomes a place of refuge for us, a shelter from the storms of life. We begin to realize in a very deep way that God is not out to judge or condemn us, but to listen and be with us, no matter what.

You may not have looked at it this way before, but prayer in its purest form is the genuine expression of our hearts before God. Whether it's with shouts of joy and praise or of bitterness and pain, prayer is the act of getting out the reality of where we are and what we're going through with our Maker. Even if you have no idea how to put what you're feeling into words, just allowing yourself to sit in His presence aides in your healing. Romans 8:26 tells us, "In the same way the Holy Spirit helps us in our weaknesses. We do not know what we ought to pray for, but the Spirit himself intercedes for us with such feeling that it cannot be expressed in words." Don't worry about how you sound or how everything is worded. Just start.

START LISTENING

Genuine engagement also involves listening. "Huh?" you may say. "How am I supposed to listen to God? Last time I checked He doesn't seem to just show up and start talking to people."

Well, yes and no. While sometimes people hear God in an audible voice (think Moses, Jesus, etc.), there are many, many ways to begin listening for and sensing God's presence and direction in your life. God will strive to connect with you in ways that are as varied as He is. He will speak to you through the Bible, certainly, which is why you should read it, but also through song and nature, other people, unique circumstances, and even in your own heart and mind. His voice can often sound like your own, nudging you to do something more. Or it can be in that quiet confidence you find when you just *know* you've made the right decision. Learning to listen to those nudges is how we begin to hear God's voice.

When you choose to follow God, He gives you the Holy Spirit, which is like a piece of God that lives inside of you and guides you. Jesus says (John 14:26), "The Holy Spirit ... will teach you all things and will remind you of everything I have said to you." I remember when I was first grabbing hold of what this meant in my life. I was going through so much; I knew I needed God's help. So, I started getting real, and I started asking God to guide me.

The very first "nudge" I got was really just an idea that wiggled its way into my head. I was walking to meet a client for lunch. Keep in mind that money was incredibly tight for me at this time, and I already knew the client would likely expect me to pick up the tab. I walked by a homeless couple sitting on the sidewalk. *You should buy them lunch.* It was a thought, in my own voice, but not a thought I would've chosen to come up with on my own, especially at that time.

Now, my first inclination was to reason the idea away because of my miniscule budget. But I knew I had been praying very specifically the previous few months about listening to God's direction, however small. I told God if it was truly Him asking me to do this, let the couple still be around after I finished lunch with my client. If so, I would bring lunch over to them. Sure enough, they were there, and I bought them lunch. End of story. The clouds didn't part. The angels didn't break into song. Yet I felt a sense of joy for not only helping someone else, but also for starting to listen to and trust God in even this small way.

That tiny step became the first toward a much larger journey. The more I learned to listen in small ways, the more God continued to direct me. And the more I followed through, the more He started directing me in bigger ways, too.

I had to put aside my very natural fear of, "What if I get it wrong? What if I'm not hearing correctly?" God is a good God. He knows my heart, and He knows when my goal is simply to listen to and trust in Him. If I tell my kids to go upstairs and go to their beds, but when I go upstairs I find them standing on their heads, will I get mad? Of course not. I may giggle, but I'm going to be proud of them for doing their best to listen to and obey me. Jesus says (Matthew 7:11), "If you know how to give good gifts … how much more so your father in heaven?" In other words, just as we would honor our children's efforts, God honors His children's efforts, too.

The other question I still consistently ask myself is, "What if it's not really God doing the talking?" After all, the Bible makes clear that Satan masquerades as an angel of light (2 Corinthians 11:14), posing as God in our hearts and minds. There are also times when I wonder if I just want something so badly that I'm managing to convince myself that it's God telling me I should have it or do it when it's really my own desire. These are valid concerns, and important ones to always keep within sight.

The Bible actually explains to us how we can know. If something really comes from God, that something will happen. No exceptions (Deuteronomy 18:21-22). God will never ask us to do something that goes against the Bible (Galatians 1:8). God's will is always clear; you will not feel confusion, even though you may not always understand *why* He's calling you to do something. There's a sense of certainty (1 Corinthians 14:33). Remember, too, God blesses obedience (1 Samuel 15:22 and Psalm 128:1). So even if you don't understand the whys, if what you're receiving isn't against the Bible, take action. I have seen how time and time again God blesses a heart that is striving to listen to His voice. The more we do so, the more we begin to recognize that it's God nudging us versus something else. Hebrews 4:7 tells us, "Today, if you hear his voice, do not harden your hearts." Keep your heart and mind open to God's direction.

Another way is to put what you're given to the test (1 John 4:1). When I bought lunch for the homeless couple that day, I wasn't sure if God was asking me to or not. So, I asked Him to allow the couple to still be there after I ate, if it was His will. They were there. Asking for confirmation can be helpful, and there's a great example of it in the book of Judges, with a guy called Gideon. God asked him to do some remarkable but very scary, overwhelming things (start an army, attack an enemy—big stuff). He asked for some very specific signs and God came through (Judges 6:36-40). But be careful! We're also reminded to not constantly put God to the test or to need signs (Luke 4:12). Sometimes God wants us to simply step out in faith. Our challenge is to listen, especially when we're in times of deep refining.

When you sense something bigger than yourself leading you, begin to take notice, no matter how small the signals are. Be wise, yes. Discern if it's God's voice or not. But the more you do so, the more you'll hear His spirit guiding you. We are told Jesus is a good shepherd and, "his sheep follow him because they know his voice … I know my sheep and my sheep know me … they too will listen to my voice" (John 10:4,14,16). This is why it's so important to slow down enough to take the time to tune in.

The ultimate benefit from genuine engagement through sharing and listening is that you will begin to connect with God in powerful, transformative ways. When you look up to God and strive to connect with him, you will start to sense His Spirit of love and compassion reaching out to you. In time, His confidence in your success will feel so strong it can almost be tangibly touched. You will begin to receive the peace only He can give washing over you, taking away the fear, anger, regret and doubt and filling you with strength, trust, confidence and belief. You can take hold of His hand and begin to allow Him to lead you out of the tunnel and back into His glorious light. You will feel centered, strengthened. It's this type of connection you're striving for.

BARRIERS TO CONNECTION

You and I both know, however, that it doesn't always feel that way. One of the hardest challenges I still face is when I don't sense God's presence in my life in a tangible way. And I have found that for all of us there are many reasons why. Skepticism can get in our way because we feel He let us down in the past, and we can't trust him. Or our view is clouded by anger because we feel like we tried it His way and it was a colossal failure. At other times, we feel so deeply ashamed of the ways we have treated God and others through our actions, our words, or our hearts, that our guilt is screaming so loudly we can't really focus on God's true face before us. And, of course, there are times we look up and sense nothing. Then we just give up on God, doing with our lives whatever we see fit, often with disastrous consequences.

Distorting our view of God is one of the best tactics the enemy ever invented. After all, if we blame God how can we see He is actually the one who can help us? If we are full of anger, then there's no way we can trust Him. If our guilt and shame somehow morph into God's voice, full of condemnation and judgment, how will we ever feel worthy enough to grab a hold of his hand? If we don't sense God's presence, it is easier to quit trying and walk away. We stay trapped in our own self-reliance. If we can be kept from genuinely seeing the true face of God when we look up, chances are high we'll just look right back down again, more depressed, angry and discouraged than when we started. Worse, it can morph into bitterness since it seems like God has failed us yet again.

Learning to deal with the barriers that keep you from seeing God's face is one of the most crucial steps to genuine connection. Breaking down those walls allows the true face of God to be seen, which in turn allows you to receive and return His love. So let's tackle these barriers one at a time. You will be surprised by how quickly the walls will crumble once you invite God into that space.

DEALING WITH ANGER & MISTRUST

It's a strange thing, being angry with God. If you're actively trying to walk with Him, you feel guilty because you know intellectually that it's wrong and He's not to blame, but you also feel very justified in your anger. If this whole "God thing" is newer to you, anger drives away your fledgling faith and belief; you start to feel like you've been duped.

My own anger toward God almost always begins when I really need Him to show up in the middle of a very hard spot, and for some reason in my mind He doesn't. He just doesn't seem to be there. And some very challenging, very hard, sometimes very bad things happen in that moment, so I become bitter and angry.

I believe in God; I pray to God. I try to center my life around God because I love Him. My love stems from His very deep, very real love for me. The truth is I expect Him to show up. I do! I know God has His own timing, and that He may be acting in ways I can't see at the moment, that there is a deeper purpose at work in my life that isn't always clear to me. But when I'm in the midst of that challenging moment, I don't care about all of that. I just don't. I don't sense God's presence showing up to help and I'm mad about it.

When I'm hurting, angry and impatient, especially when prayers aren't answered in my timing, when my prescribed "formula" of how I think things should work between God and me fails, I struggle with anger and disconnection. I struggle with blaming God. It doesn't matter that I can intellectualize that it isn't His fault. Anger is what I *feel*.

The hard truth is I have found it never goes well for me when I give in and let my emotions get the best of me. There's the perverse joy that comes from a "backatcha" moment, but it's short lived. I've learned the only person you hurt and get back at when you go crazy is yourself. You're the one that will have to deal with the hangover, the "drunk dial" call that should never have been made, the police, the person you wake up next to, the bills that have now grown because you spent what you didn't have to begin with, etc. That delicious piece of cake tastes really good those first few bites. Twenty bites later, however, you are no longer really tasting the cake; you're biting into your own bitterness and anger. It's the consequences from those moments that can be truly devastating.

Let's take it even deeper. Your "ex" is acting like a jerk again. The kids are hurting, crying even. The ex-spouse acts clueless or, worse yet, extremely justified in the bad behavior. Anyone from the outside looking in would say, "What a complete jerk. I can't believe they get away with this. You should [insert well-intentioned but terrible, reactionary advice here]." Oh, how truly great it would feel to just let loose and scream everything your ex needs to hear. Besides, every sharp word, every insult and slam you deliver would be the absolute truth. No one would argue that he or she doesn't deserve it. Okay, so maybe that's not the best way to try and change the situation, but it sure feels great at that moment, right? Hmm. Not really.

You see, you still have to live with the consequences of your actions. God's grace, mercy and forgiveness are always there for you, but those consequences remain. When you act out in hurtful ways, however justified you are, you fuel the fire of ugliness instead of quenching it. Those words, that bad decision you've already made, are still out there. When we forget to slow down and remember God and instead choose to react, the barriers the enemy builds just get thicker and higher. And our anger toward God grows because our situation isn't getting better; it's getting worse.

Internal anger can be just as damaging. At this point in my life, I've learned to not outwardly react, so most of my anger is internal. While the consequences of my anger may be less obvious to the outside observer, they're still there. I stop listening. I can't hear God's voice, or even if I do, I shut it out. I begin to feel alone, abandoned. My steps are less sure. My connections with others begin to suffer. Worse, I start making decisions based on what *I* think is good.

So how do we stop the negative pattern of blaming God and instead begin to turn to Him for healing? I think it starts with realizing first and foremost that our anger is okay. The Bible puts it this way (Ephesians 4:26-27): "Go ahead and be angry. You do well to be angry—but don't use your anger as fuel for revenge. And don't stay angry. Don't go to bed angry. Don't give the Devil that kind of foothold in your life." It's all right to be angry at your circumstances, angry with the person who's hurting you, angry at injustice. God hates those things, too. That's why He sent Jesus to die—someone has to pay the penalty for those sins.

Where we get into trouble is when we decide we should be the ones passing out the punishment, that we have to make that person pay. Remember, Jesus died for you as well. Your sins, your mistakes, your bad decisions—every wrong move you've ever made. Ever. And he didn't die for you when you were trying to get your act together. Quite the opposite! In Romans 5:8 we're told, "But God put his love on the line for us by offering his Son in sacrificial death while we were of no use whatever to him." In the midst of your darkest moment, Jesus died for you because of his deep, unchanging love for you.

No matter how good you may view yourself as being, you are never good enough to somehow earn your place with God. In His eyes, "there is no one on earth who is righteous, no one who does what is right and never sins" (Ecclesiastes 7:20). That's why He says in Hebrews 10:30, "It is mine to avenge; I will repay," and again, "The Lord will judge his people." It's because we're in no position to be justified in making other people pay. We can pursue them legally and with every allowable means, but lashing out in anger and condemning them in our hearts comes back to bite us. We are the ones who suffer. In Matthew 7:2, Jesus says, "For in the same way you judge others, you will be judged, and with the measure you use, it will be measured to you." No one is worth risking your soul for. No one!

The best scripture I have found that really helps me when it seems like I'm getting all the bad breaks is in Psalm 73:

My feet had almost slipped; I had nearly lost my foothold for I envied the arrogant and wicked when I saw their prosperity. They have no struggles; their bodies are healthy and strong. They are free from common burdens; they are not plagued by human ills. They're proud and violent. From their callous hearts comes sin and their evil imaginations have no limits. They scoff, speak with malice, and threaten oppression. They say, "How would God know? Does the Most High know anything?" Surely in vain I have kept my heart pure and tried to do right. Every morning brings new punishments. Yet if I had spoken out like that, I would have betrayed your children. When I tried to understand all this, it troubled me deeply till I entered His sanctuary and realized something so chilling and final: their lives have a deadly end because You have certainly set the wicked upon a slippery slope; You've set them up to slide to their destruction. And they won't see it coming. It will happen so fast; Yet I am always with you; you hold me by my right hand. You guide me with your counsel, and afterward you will take me into glory. God is the strength of my heart and my portion forever.

God will deal with the other guy. You are accountable for one person and one person only: You. Once you come to terms with who you are before God and remember it's His job to fix people, not yours, it's much easier to give grace to others. There will be a judgment, but by God's grace we can be forgiven, move forward, let go and heal.

What if you view the other guy as being God? In your anger you find yourself yelling, "*Why did God allow my spouse to die?*" Or, "*How can a loving God allow this to happen?*" Or, "*I've tried to do my best for God and this is how he repays me?!*" Once again, remind yourself of the truth: We live in a fallen, broken world. We've been given choice. God didn't make us mindless robots programmed to obey. He made us living, breathing, thinking and feeling individuals who are allowed to make our own choices, good or bad. Sometimes your bad choices have a negative impact on others. Sometimes others' bad choices have a negative impact on you. You can't have one without the other. You can't have one person judged immediately by God but then not yourself. It just doesn't work that way.

The truth is while we're on this earth, we will never fully understand the whys behind what happens. God tells us in Isaiah 55:8, "My intentions are not always yours, and I do not go about things as you do." There are things that are just beyond us. Again, reminding ourselves of God's truths during these times of stretching—His love for us endures forever; He never leaves or forsakes us, etc.—helps to remind us that while we may not get it, God can put a purpose to it, even if it's simply to take your loved one home to a better place where there are no tears, no pain, no fear and no trials. Heaven.

The other thing I would add about holding on to negative emotion is that the person who is most hurt by it is you. I guarantee no one else is losing sleep over your anger and bitterness. Only you. So let it go. Trust that

God is in control. Know that He has your back, even when you don't sense or see it. As your faith and understanding of this grows, so will your ability to actually feel God's presence, and the angry haze will begin to dissipate.

DEALING WITH GUILT

Guilt is a tricky thing. On the one hand, guilt is sort of hard-wired into us to help us know when something is off. It's that helpful niggling in the heart and mind that forces us to really analyze who we are and what we're doing, and to make better choices. It reminds us of the apology we keep putting off, or pushes us toward that act of kindness we need to do. This is a good type of guilt that works like a compass and helps us stay on track.

But there is also a bad type of guilt, the type that grabs you by the jugular and won't let go long after you've changed and moved forward. It's the kind of guilt that tells you you're no good, you never were, and you never will be. It's the guilt that refuses to allow you to feel forgiven, whole, healed, and precious in God's sight. It's the guilt that crushes you underfoot instead of propelling you forward. Sometimes we confuse that ugly guilt with the voice of God.

Remember how I said the enemy loves to build walls between God and us? How much better if he can convince us the negative voice we hear in our head *is* God. Again, 2 Corinthians 11:14 warns us, "Satan masquerades as an angel of light." In other words, he likes to make it seem like he's God, telling us how horrible we are and that we can't change. If you've come from a very harsh, dogmatic and/or ritualistic religious background, especially in a church that really emphasizes sin and judgment at the expense of grace and mercy, you likely struggle with this.

God does want us to acknowledge our sin for what it is, repent and move forward—all concepts we'll talk about under intentionality. He sent His Son to die for sin once and for all so we would no longer be bound by it. Galatians 5:1 tells us, "It is for freedom that Christ has set us free. Stand firm, then, and do not let yourselves be burdened again by a yoke of slavery." He doesn't want us to be enslaved to guilt, but to walk in freedom and forgiveness, not because we've earned it somehow, but because it is God's loving gift to us through Jesus.

Again, the key is to replace the lies with truth. The lie is you can't change and you can't be forgiven. God's truth is quite different. He says (Isaiah 43), "You are precious and honored in my sight … [so] do not be afraid for I am with you." He adds, "Forget the former things; do not dwell on the past. See, I am doing a new thing! Now it springs up in you. Do you not perceive it?" He sent His Son to die for you so you *can* be forgiven! When the negative tape starts playing, read scriptures that give you a different story, the *true* story.

I'm sure you've heard someone say (or maybe said yourself), "If I walked into that church the ceiling would fall on me," meaning that sinners don't belong there. Well, let me tell ya—if church buildings were literally going to fall down because someone with a lot of sin walked inside, there wouldn't be a church in this world left standing. We all fall short. No one is better than you before God, and no one is worse. Romans 3:23 says, "We all have sinned and fall short of the glory of God." You don't have a corner on that market. Neither do I. We are the same before God, and we all have the opportunity to move forward toward strength and healing with Him if we choose.

There are great examples of this in the Bible, both Old and New Testament. King David, described as a man after God's own heart, committed adultery with the wife of one of his top commanders. When he found out she was pregnant and he couldn't get her husband to sleep with her to cover it up, he sent the man to certain death on the battlefield so he could quickly marry the woman. I'd say that's pretty messy.

Paul, who became the most influential man in the early church, started out tracking down Christians and killing them because of their faith. Imagine if he'd killed your brother, later became a Christian, and then you had to sit down and listen to him give a sermon several years later.

There are prostitutes and thieves, liars and murderers, adulterers and everything in between that we find being healed from the inside out, making a turn-around in their lives and moving forward in powerful ways. No matter what it is you've done or how guilty you feel, you are not the only one, nor will you be the last one. Quit letting the lies beat you up and remember you, even you, are loved and redeemable.

DEALING WITH NOTHINGNESS

There are two key reasons we can feel a sense of emptiness when we look up at God. One is simply because we don't know Him yet. This whole God thing is new to us, and we're not sure how to begin to build a genuine, engaged relationship with Him. The other is because we feel so burned out, so worn and spent that we literally have nothing left inside, no emotion or hope, period.

Let's tackle both.

If you've never really known much about God, or it's just been a really long time since you tried, take heart. It's never too late to begin learning how to connect with Him. Begin putting into place what we've discussed so far and you will start to sense His presence and direction in your life. Be patient.

Like anything important, it is a process. I've included some suggestions for you at the end of this chapter to help you get started.

When we're feeling empty because of life's circumstances, finding motivation is hard. We're like a car that's run out of gas—it takes tremendous effort to get it moving forward again. The biggest challenge is we lack any energy to even want to try. We've simply given up and quit.

I have had seasons in life where even the strength to get up out of bed eluded me, where I just didn't care about anything anymore. I'd try to get some motivation and move forward, but it would quickly fade and I'd drift back to being depressed and numb. I used to think of it as this slimy pit that would always suck me back in no matter how hard I tried to get out of it. I'll never forget the first time I read this scripture in Psalm 40:2: "He lifted me out of the slimy pit, out of the mud and mire; he set my feet on a rock and gave me a firm place to stand."

I couldn't believe it. I just cried. It was the first time I began to have an inkling of hope that even though *I* couldn't change me, God could. I started to pray for the desire to want to even *want* to try. I started reading a lot of the Psalms and a lot of the Bible (Psalms 102 & 103 are a great place to start—they're short so you can read them back-to-back). I began to talk with God, even though it felt really weird and awkward at first. Most importantly, I began to look for those negative tapes and lies that were playing over and over again in my head, and slowly replacing them with truth.

It took time. It took some professional help at points, something I highly encourage if you need it. But slowly and steadily, not always consistently and not always in a forward direction, but over time I began to move forward, re-engage, and re-gain hope and vision for my life. I began to connect with God and the world at large on an emotional level again. He truly did put me on a firm place to stand. And He can do it for you. Simply start, no matter how pointless it feels.

DEALING WITH SELF-RELIANCE

You know those times where you literally feel like you're crawling out of your skin? Where you just want something to happen, and you want it to happen NOW! You can't settle your mind. You can't relax. You can't find joy. You're itching for something to change or to have a response immediately. It's difficult to remember to turn to God during these times. You just feel so desperate, so frustrated, so needy.

I find I always want to try and take control of the situation, to find my solution instead of falling to my knees, crying out and waiting for God's solution. I'm not good at waiting, frankly. I don't like to wait. I'm a child of our microwave society—I want it hot, fast and now. I'm that person that gets impatient at the drive-through if I have to wait more than thirty seconds to get my food. And if I'm asked to pull aside so they can bring me my items because they're not quite ready yet, watch out! I guarantee you I'm feeling pretty ugly about it.

Why? Why do I do that? Why do *we* do that? When I make myself stop and think about it, I realize that if I was home cutting up those potatoes, making that hamburger patty, or worse yet processing chicken parts into shapes to be breaded and deep fried, I'd be waiting on me for a very long time. Those two or three minutes I had to wait would stretch into twenty or thirty minutes easily. I would even have to clean up the kitchen afterwards. So I should be grateful, but instead I'm this angry, impatient creature who wants, wants, wants, and all on my timing.

The thing is, when I just go it on my own I find my solutions are never as thorough, never as effective as God's. It's not that I'm ineffective at making good decisions. God gave me a brain to use and He expects me to use it. And I do. But there are times when I know God is asking me to lean into Him a bit deeper in a specific situation. I don't sense Him telling me to move forward, but I move forward anyway. That's what self-reliance is all about.

Society doesn't help. We're told "Time is Money," that the clock is ticking so we better get the ball rolling. As Nike tells us, "Just do it." God is so very different. What God seems to value most in scripture is our relationship with Him and the growth of our characters carved out with His patience and love over time. That can feel very counter-cultural in a society that values speed.

So how do we slow down? How do we stop in order to make time for connection with God? Maybe more importantly, why should we bother if we don't see the benefits right away? Fair questions.

Romans 8:28 tells us, "And we know that in all things God works for the good of those who love him." God will work through what you and I are going through to help us grow, even the ugly things. Now it may not happen in our timing or in the way we think it should, but that doesn't change the fact that He's actively working for our good. Sometimes we need to step back and remember God is in control, and that He will show up in ways we don't always understand, recognize or appreciate initially. Read that sentence again.

Just because situations don't go the way we anticipate or expect doesn't mean God has left us in the dust. Even when you don't feel God's presence, it doesn't change the fact He's still there. In 2 Timothy 2:13 it says, "If we are faithless, He remains faithful, for He cannot disown Himself." Even if you and I are shut down, closed up, feeling exposed and completely alone, God is by our side waiting for us to notice Him beside us. He is already reaching out to help whether we sense it or not.

There is a George MacDonald quote I love that really helps me with this: "[God] may be approaching our consciousness from behind, coming forward through the regions of our darkness into our light, long before we begin to be aware that he is answering our request—has answered it and is visiting His child." Sometimes the best thing we can do is simply stop the craziness, stop the frenetic pace, look up from our ashes and acknowledge the Lord is standing right there beside us. Beside *you*.

Slow down. Make time to connect. It doesn't have to be this big, formal thing. It can be as you're driving, while you're showering, over your morning coffee, throughout your workout—literally anytime and anywhere. Simply putting it before God every day and asking Him to guide and help you is a great start. As He reminds us in Psalm 46:10, "Be still, and know that I am God."

Know as well that leaning into God isn't a crutch. It takes more strength, more integrity, and more determination to lean into God for answers than to just go off and do what seems right to you. Begin to develop your spiritual muscle by looking to Him for your answers instead of rushing ahead into your next tunnel.

Realize that you are an important piece of this beautiful tapestry God is weaving together. You may not always understand why you zig one way and then the other, but He's got the big picture and knows the work of art He is creating with your personal stories. Proverbs 3:5-6 tells us, "Trust God from the bottom of your heart; don't try to figure out everything on your own. Listen for God's voice in everything you do, everywhere you go; He's the one who will keep you on track."

MOVING FORWARD

Any discussion about barriers that keep us from God would be incomplete without adding an important point: The broken pieces in you will keep trying to rebuild those walls once they're torn down. You and I won't reach some constant emotional nirvana with God while we're on this Earth. We will begin to recognize when we are in step with God, certainly. Those times of bliss and joy will grow in number and in length. We will also begin to notice when construction has started on a new wall in our hearts and lives. The more we learn to connect with God, the faster we'll sense those things and not settle for anything less than genuine connection. But it doesn't keep the old barriers from trying to resurface.

Jesus prepares us for this when He tells us (Luke 11:24-26), "When a corrupting spirit comes out of a man, it goes through arid places seeking rest and does not find it. Then it says, 'I will return to the house I left.' When it arrives, it finds the house swept clean and put in order. Then it goes and takes seven other spirits more wicked than itself, and they go in and live there. And the final condition of that man is worse than the first."

Jesus isn't telling us we're condemned to have things go even worse if we begin cleaning up our spiritual house. He's reminding us of why it's so important to stay connected to Him as we do so. Just prior to saying this, He tells us in verse 23, "He who is not with me is against me, and he who does not gather with me, scatters." In other words, He's making it clear that while the negative gunk will try to reassert itself in our minds and hearts to try to break and scatter us, if we connect into His strength, He will protect us. A few sermons later (Luke 12:6-7) He reminds us, "Are not five sparrows sold for two pennies? Yet not one of them is forgotten by God. Indeed, the very hairs of your head are all numbered. Don't be afraid; you are worth more than many sparrows." Keep fighting to genuinely connect.

SUMMARY

Let's recap. Step 1 to connection is to realize God is there, He loves you, and He wants to have a relationship with you. The next step is to surrender your masks. Acknowledge God. Share your hurt and your fears with Him. Engage with God in a real, genuine way. Don't be afraid to be you—the good, the bad and the ugly. God will take it all.

Then, begin to listen for His voice in new and deeper ways. Authentic engagement equals connection. Be aware of the barriers that can keep you from hearing Him and ask God to start knocking them down. Remember 2 Cor. 10:5, which says, "We use our powerful God-tools for smashing warped philosophies, tearing down barriers erected against the truth of God, fitting every loose thought and emotion and impulse into the structure of life shaped by Christ."

Finally, remember your relationship with God is a constant, ongoing cycle of surrender. You will not be able to perfectly connect with God 24/7. Just remember God *is* there 24/7 even when you don't feel it. Take the time you need to step aside and allow Him to show up. In time, it will feel like coming home.

FOR FURTHER THOUGHT

1. What is a way you're hearing from God right now about your situation?
2. What are you learning about yourself?
3. What is your biggest challenge to connecting with God?
4. What is a possible solution?
5. Go to God at least once this week in a deeper way than you have for a while. If you've never spent time alone with God before, set aside some time to do so. Go outside or to a church or to a quiet space—anywhere that helps you feel emotionally connected to God—and spend special time with Him. Be real. Get your issues out with Him. Once you've done this, write down how you felt afterwards.

IF THIS WHOLE 'GOD THING' IS NEW TO YOU

Start by reading one of the first four books of the New Testament, called the Gospels (Matthew, Mark, Luke, and John). They will give you a great overview of Jesus' life, the lessons He taught, how He interacted with people, etc. It's a great place to start. As you read, ask yourself what you're learning about Jesus and God, especially their character and their heart for you.

There are also all sorts of devotional guides out there at bookstores and on the internet that will help you start studying through the Bible so you can understand God more clearly. I recommend one that focuses on God's enduring love for you and the type of relationship He wants to develop with you. Sales clerks at Christian bookstores are often knowledgeable about what they have in stock and can point you in the right direction.

Finally, you may want to consider finding a church to attend if you don't do so already. There is no such thing as a perfect church since by definition it's filled with imperfect people—including you and me. Yet we are wired to need people, and finding a group that not only understands your struggles, but can also help you along on your journey is worth the effort.

CHAPTER 4

FIRST STEPS
Bravery

"Success is not final; failure is not fatal: it is the courage to continue that counts."
— Winston Churchill

Think of all the movies and books out there with the word "brave" in the title. There's *Braveheart, Brave, Home of the Brave,* and *Brave New World* just to name a few. If we then added all of the movies and books that have bravery as their theme, that would be a seriously long list! Bravery is one of the words we love. It brings to mind greatness, victory. When I watch these movies or read these books, it seems there's always someone who is brave in the face of tremendous challenge, who unfailingly sticks to a greater purpose and vision and never wavers in their belief, even when everyone else around them does. They have integrity and honor. They never fail. I sit up a little straighter when I hear about them. It makes me want to be a better person.

I wish I could be one of those people. I really do. I want to be that fearless warrior who demolishes the enemy against tremendous odds and comes out on top; I want to be the one who, even in failure, has such unshakeable faith in my cause that those around me are inspired. But the truth is I'm not. I *do* fail; I waver in my vision and in my belief in what can be. My faith falters. I suspect yours does, too.

Guess what? We're in good company. One of my favorite characters in the Bible is Moses. Why? Because he doubts and wavers like I do. When God calls him to do extraordinary things, Moses doesn't snap to attention, jump in and start making history. Instead, his first response is, "But why me? What makes you think that I could ever go to Pharaoh and lead the children of Israel out of Egypt?" (Exodus 3:11).

So, God tells Moses He'll be with him. He reveals to Moses the name He wants to be called by His people and gives him very specific direction on exactly how to move forward with this vision. Does Moses finally get excited? No. He comes back with, "They won't trust me. They won't listen to a word I say. They're going to say, 'God? Appear to him? Hardly!'" (Exodus 4:1).

God then does a few miracles for Moses and lets him know He will give Moses special powers to use (how cool is that?). But does our man Moses finally understand God is on his side, find faith, and start taking steps forward? No. He begins to make excuses about how he isn't a very good speaker and how he's actually kinda slow. God encourages Moses again and tells him He'll give Moses the words and teach him what to say.

Okay, at this point even I would begin to believe God had some pretty remarkable plans laid out for me and would really hold my hand and grant me tremendous victory. Yet this is why I love Moses. He doesn't say, "Woohoo, God! Let's go!" Instead, he says, "Please, Lord, I beg you to send Your message through someone else, anyone else" (Exodus 4:13).

Even then, God doesn't change His mind about Moses. He gets angry, yes. He tells him He'll let his brother Aaron come along and speak on Moses' behalf. But He never withdraws His vision for Moses. Nearly two entire chapters of the Bible are devoted to God trying to convince Moses He's with him (that's a huge amount of biblical real estate—most of the others we read about who are called by God get a few sentences or a paragraph at best). And Moses is still skeptical. I can relate to that. And interestingly, Aaron never does speak on Moses' behalf to the people. Moses does all the speaking. God just told Moses what he needed to hear in the moment.

I think we're all a lot like Moses. We want to be more like the William Wallace we see in the movie *Braveheart*, but in reality we, like Moses, question God; we don't want to understand and ultimately we don't want to go down the road that lays before us—even when we finally get that it's the right road. Obviously, Moses did some amazing, remarkable things and became one of our greatest Bible legends. That's why I like him. He reminds me that God will still do miraculous things in my life even when I have a hard time believing Him, or struggle to get myself and my fears out of God's way.

There is a quote I love from the book *Allegiant* by Veronica Roth. It says:

There are so many ways to be brave in this world. Sometimes bravery involves laying down your life for something bigger than yourself, or for someone else. Sometimes it involves giving up everything you have ever known, or everyone you have ever loved, for the sake of something greater.

But sometimes it doesn't.

Sometimes it is nothing more than gritting your teeth through pain, and the work of every day, the slow walk toward a better life.

That is the sort of bravery I must have now.

So, let's explore what day-to-day bravery looks like—not the William Wallace bravery but the messy, not always straightforward, sometimes wavering bravery of Moses. I have personally experienced and now believe this kind of daily bravery will bring about many little miracles in your life that, over time, combine to become the most important miracle of all—the joy and peace that comes from a transformed, boldly shining life.

If Connection is about being willing to express our mess with God, Bravery is about being willing to work through our mess with Him. Being real, acknowledging where you're at and what you're going through is a big part of bravery. This can feel counter-intuitive because our egos tell us to define ourselves by what we achieve, to tie our security and confidence to our performance. When we face big obstacles, our performance falters and so does our sense of self. But you are not your circumstances. You are a child of God.

Remember when your self-worth is tied into God's unconditional, never ending love for you, you begin to realize you're precious, valued and loved, regardless of what your achievements are or how others perceive you. This is where God's "peace that passes understanding" comes into place, where "perfect love drives out fear." You're no longer bound by your shame of messing up, of making mistakes, of failure, or by your achievement and success, and whether or not you can handle it. Your strength comes from your internal power source—from God. God values *you*—period. There are no conditions; no limits. He doesn't care how messy you are. He simply loves you.

When Moses was arguing with God, what he was really doing was being brave enough to connect with God and be messy, to work through his fears and his weaknesses. Now God already knew all of these things about Moses, but that didn't change the fact Moses needed to wrestle through these issues with the Big Man for himself. He had to embrace his new circumstances. He had to face his fears.

Negative fear, in fact, is the biggest deterrent to our ability to move forward and the biggest barrier we face. Now don't get me wrong—we can have healthy fear that motivates us to want to change. (What if I'm stuck here forever? What if I lose my family? etc.) It can be a good starting point. But negative fear saps us of strength, drive and determination. It tells us we can't change, we never could and we never will. It takes our eyes off of God and fixes them squarely on our circumstances. Moses kept pointing out his circumstances and weaknesses; God kept reminding Moses He was with him so there was nothing Moses couldn't do or overcome. Eventually, reluctantly, Moses chose to believe God and slowly move forward.

A great beginning question to ask yourself as you start tackling your own messiness is how did you end up inside your tunnel? For some people, they know the exact answer. Or at least they think they do. For others, they have no idea. I asked a good friend once how she got into the spot she was in emotionally. She replied, looking dazed, "I have no idea. All I know is I'm unhappy and unfulfilled. I feel restless all the time, and I don't really know what to do or how to change it."

Sometimes we're thrust into a tunnel through traumatic life circumstances; sometimes it's been a slowly developing wound in our hearts and lives. Or it can be an issue we should have dealt with long ago but we ignored, hoping it would somehow magically go away, only to watch it fester and grow until it became something even more challenging and toxic. Regardless of the "how," we need to do some initial assessing in order to begin taking those first tentative steps forward.

TRAUMA

Think of trauma as being similar to a car-wreck victim. When someone who has been hurt in an accident is taken into the ER, it's pretty obvious to everyone why the person is there. Many of his wounds are out there for everyone to see. Yet there could be many secondary injuries, much less obvious to the naked eye but every bit as lethal and dangerous. It's these underlying causes or issues that put you at risk of not seeing clearly what needs to be healed. Divorce, abuse, death, and adultery are all examples of traumatic events capable of immediately placing you in a challenging tunnel against your will. The guilt and resentment you may feel are just a few of those underlying causes that can come back to bite you, regardless of why.

As we look at underlying issues together, remember it's not about judgment, making you feel horrible or assigning blame. Taking a hard look at yourself can be tough, especially when you're thrust into circumstances beyond your control. What happened may not be your fault, but your response—how you're moving forward and dealing with your heart and emotions about it—is in your hands.

The truth is there's only one person you have control over—and that's you. You can't change anyone but yourself. Whether you crashed your own car or someone crashed into you—hard and intentionally—never let go of the fact that you do have a choice in how you handle it and you are worth being healed. Isaiah tells us that God "tends his flock like a shepherd; He gathers the lambs in his arms and carries them close to his heart; he gently leads those that have young" (Isaiah 40:11). God not only wants to help lead you past what has happened, but to grow *through* your ugly, awful experience in a way that empowers you and helps you steer clear of similar painful situations in the future.

In addressing underlying causes in your life, you have to look beyond the obvious. If you're going through divorce, for instance, the obvious upfront reason for it could be because you or your spouse cheated. The less obvious reason may be the way you've treated your spouse all the way through the marriage, or the way you've allowed yourself to be treated. Divorce rarely happens in a void. It involves two flawed people who both have made mistakes. What are yours? How did you get to this point on *your* end? Those are the types of questions you need to begin asking yourself if you're truly going to understand the tunnel you find yourself in.

Even if your spouse is one of those rare individuals who is truly evil, the kind of person God describes as having a "depraved mind, to do what ought not to be done ... filled with every kind of wickedness, evil, greed and depravity ... they invent ways of doing evil" (Romans 1:28-30), there is still some exploring for you to do. Why did you allow yourself to enter into a relationship with this person? If you've stayed in ugly circumstances over time, why? If you dig in deeply, you'll begin to realize it's not just because of the kids, much as they do matter. You may have issues of self-worth to wrestle with, or dysfunctional boundaries in place, or even a misplaced sense of loyalty. While these are hard issues to admit to and face, they are the very keys to your emotional healing and to keep you from repeating these patterns in the future.

Even something as heart wrenching as death can have underlying problems hiding between a very natural and normal heartache and grief. Do you have unresolved issues with the person who passed? It could be anger, hurt or bitterness toward how he or she treated you. It could be those very same emotions toward yourself about how you treated that person. Trust issues with God, often tied to let-downs from the past, can easily enter in, too. Beginning to explore what those issues are is an important start.

Remember—the more you understand what it is you need to grow in and heal from, the less likely you are to continue to be defined by those issues in the future. You are worth so much more than your circumstances. Don't be afraid to dig deeper, even when you feel resentful about having to do so. "Trust in the Lord with all your heart and lean not on your own understanding; in all your ways acknowledge him and He will make your paths straight" (Proverbs 3:5-6).

SLOW-GROWING WOUND

A tunnel of this nature starts off almost imperceptibly small. Like a slow growing tumor, you may not notice the effects right away. For most of us, we find ourselves in this tunnel through an accumulation of one poor choice here, something we avoided over there, and over time all of these individual decisions and disappointments evolve into one dark, challenging tunnel. You realize you're miserable and unhappy, but you're not sure why.

Probably more than any other tunnel, finding yourself in one with no understanding of how you got there requires some time to really assess your heart, your choices, who you are, and where you're headed. You will need to evaluate how you feel about yourself, your key relationships, your work, and possibly even your past. You may find one area that really glares back at you, or it may be a combination of a few things.

Start by looking at your relationships. What are your primary relationships like? Does your family respect and honor your personal boundaries? If you're married, are you satisfied most days in that relationship? Friendships are also important to evaluate. Do you have good, close friends you can trust and you feel supported by? What kind of friend are you to others? How do you treat others and how do you allow others to treat you? Would others agree with you? Remember—honesty is key.

Good, healthy relationships are interdependent in that they are mutually beneficial. Negative relationships lean toward codependency where one person supports or enables another person's poor choices. What kind of relationships do you consistently find yourself in? Do you put the needs of everyone else before your own God-given needs, or do you expect others to do the heavy lifting in your life for you? Remember the importance of being honest with yourself as you wrestle through this process.

Boundaries are also important. When it comes to personal boundaries, do you understand what yours are? Do you honor them and expect others to do the same? How about at work? Are you willing to respectfully take a stand for yourself if necessary, or do you sometimes bulldoze over people to get your way? Do you set realistic expectations for yourself? Would others agree with you?

Don't forget to take a close look at you. Are you able to take personal time for yourself, doing things that make you feel empowered and/or happy? Or, is your schedule dominated by what you do for yourself with no room for others? Are you willing to ask for what you need when you need it, without feeling guilty or manipulative, or do you never allow anyone else to help you? Do you allow yourself some breathing room and space within your schedule, or are you afraid that if you stop the world will crash around you? Why do you think that is? What are your eating habits like? Is there anything in your past you've never really dealt with?

While I'm sure you can think of many other questions to ask yourself, what you'll find as you start prayerfully probing a little more deeply is that God will begin to show up and give you answers. Proverbs 20:5 says, "The purposes of a person's heart are deep waters, but one who has insight draws them out." Begin exploring how you *really* feel about your life, not how you *think* you should feel or even what you tell everyone else you feel. Understanding will follow.

IGNORED WOUND

Anyone with a wound that got a lot worse before it got better will tell you they wished they had dealt with the issue much sooner; delay brought so much more pain. If you have a festering wound, you know it. You're already kicking yourself for being gullible, naïve, stubborn, stupid—or whatever your adjective is you kick yourself with. It's the issue you've pushed aside hoping it would disappear or somehow resolve on its own; the pain from your past you keep telling yourself you should be over by now but it's ruling your life. Or the person you've known you've needed to confront but instead chose to ignore, hoping he or she would just figure it out in time, but now you've got a nightmare on your hands.

If this is your tunnel, take heart. Emotional injuries that have not been dealt with upfront do require some "corrective surgery," but they can be corrected. God specializes in healing the unhealable, even if the only one healed is you and your heart. Remember Jesus' word of encouragement in Matthew 19:26, where he says, "With God all things are possible." Allow yourself the freedom to admit that while you may not have handled your challenge well initially, it doesn't stand to reason that you can't do so now. God tells us it's not the well He has come to heal, but the sick (Matthew 9:12). Acknowledging that you need help and direction is a huge first step.

Start by understanding why you may have put aside your situation in the first place. Do you hate confrontation to your own detriment? Why? Is there something from your past triggering fear whenever conversations or situations aren't running smoothly? Do you often find yourself in the middle of challenging circumstances? Why might that be? Or do you always seek ways to escape your reality, whether it's with an over-full schedule, drugs, sex, etc.? What are you afraid of facing, and why? Bravery helps you begin searching for the answers.

Another important idea to look at is your sense of worth. Do you believe God desires good things for you, that He wants you to experience His joy and peace, and that He sees you as worthwhile? Do you routinely accept less from those around you, or have unrealistic expectations you place on others? Are you happy with who you are? Do you believe you deserve to have people around you who support you and have your best interests at heart? If any of these statements stand out to you, begin to look to God to help you understand why.

Firmly resist the temptation to take the quickest route that comes to mind to escape your tunnel. Rushing into a haphazard decision will not only *not* help, it will likely make your situation worse. Yes, worse is still possible. Take the time you need to thoroughly and thoughtfully work through your tunnel with the Great Physician at your side, and despite your feelings to the contrary, you'll be amazed at what He's capable of.

BRAVE NEXT STEPS

Now that you've had a chance to explore the dark tunnel you find yourself in, let's unpack some practical ways to apply day-to-day bravery to find a way back to sunlight. Let the whole situation unfold in your mind. Don't emotionally detach from it. Start by asking yourself, what is out of your control in this situation? What do you have control over? Write these things down. Next, ask yourself how you feel in this situation. Get in touch with all of the emotions involved, good and bad. Try not to filter or analyze your feelings or thoughts. Just write them down and get them out.

Now step back and take a look at your list. How might you go about getting your feelings out with God? How can you connect with God over your list? Perhaps it's praying through it with Him. It might be carving out time to talk with Him about it in a place where you feel connection with Him. It may simply involve being still and letting God show up in your circumstances: "Be still and know I am God" (Psalm 46:10). It might involve yelling at Him, crying, complaining or whatever else needs to be expressed, however messy. Go to your Creator the way you would go to an amazing earthly dad who loves you and accepts you where you're at: "And by him we cry, 'Abba, Father.' The Spirit himself testifies with our spirit that we are God's children" (Romans 8:16-17). What might He say to you about your list?

As you look at these challenges with God, what do you want to keep control of that needs to be let go? In other words, what is firmly beyond you that needs to be placed in the Master's hands? For me, I had to realize I had no control over whether or not I would be able to stay married. I had no control over how much child support would or wouldn't come in. I couldn't control the environment my kids would be in when they were away from me. What I did have and will always have is control over my own decisions in response to those circumstances.

Was I going to yell and scream about how unfair, unjust, and wrong it all was? Would I allow myself to be swallowed up in the anguish I felt, to stay in that dark tunnel? Or would I learn to lean into God to gain His strength in order to find ways to rise above my circumstances, look for His solutions to what I could control and influence, and surrender to God what was beyond me?

Let me tell you, it ain't easy! I had times of deep grief over what was lost, times of overwhelming despair, and rightly so. Yet embracing that messiness, allowing myself my feelings while realizing that God could give me strength and courage to move forward through it all, was liberating. I began to learn how to find peace in the storms, and how to grow and evolve past what was blocking me. So don't be afraid to confront what you need to let go of.

Now let's dig in deeper. What are some fears you will have to face in this situation? They may already be represented in your list, but if not, add them now. It could be fear of failing, fear of succeeding, fear of the unknown, fear of being hurt or being exposed, fear of being worthless, fear of being abandoned, fear of never being different, or staying stuck in your tunnel. Whatever they are, write them down. Again, don't filter or analyze yet. Just get it out.

Look at your fears, take a deep breath, and pray for some insight from God, because we're diving in even deeper now. As you do, remember God's words to you: "Fear not, for I am with you. Do not be dismayed. I am your God. I will strengthen you; I will help you; I will uphold you with my victorious right hand" (Isaiah 41:10). Grab hold of His strength and look within. Where do your fears come from? What is the "why" God is trying to show you? What is at the root of your fear?

For me, two of my most consistent fears were fear of succeeding and fear of the unknown. When I look at the why behind the fear, I've had to face two key issues. When it comes to success, I struggle with believing I'm worthy enough to receive the great blessings and opportunities God wants to give me, or that He *wants* to give them to me. My lack of worth gets in the way. With fear of the unknown, it almost always comes down to my desire to be in control. I want to know the outcome and will do many things to try to manipulate my circumstances in an attempt to get the outcome I want without including God in the process.

As you explore what your root issue or issues are, take the time you need to really connect with God in your situation. It might take a few days, weeks or even months to get down to the root issue. Sometimes we may need professional help to get there. That's okay. Continuing to dig and explore is part of how you express your day-to-day, not always straightforward, messy bravery with God. Every little piece of the internal puzzle you receive is a victory. The key is to keep pushing—not into your will but into what God wants to show you.

Bravery is also about giving up your rights. Did I have a right to be angry about my circumstances? Absolutely. Was it in any way fair or just? Not at all. Remember—God never tells us we can't feel angry, or hurt, or any other emotion we may be feeling. He also makes it clear He hates the wrong that's being done to us. In Psalms 5:5-6 it says, "The arrogant cannot stand in your (God's) presence; you hate all who do wrong. You destroy those who tell lies; bloodthirsty and deceitful men the Lord abhors."

Yet God calls us to act not out of our emotion, but out of our righteousness—a fancy religious word that really means right choices or right living. While I may be justified in screaming at my ex, for example, doing so doesn't really resolve anything for the greater good. I may feel better in that moment, but when he starts yelling back or my kids get wind of the conflict, I just feel worse. God says, "In your anger do not sin" (Ephesians 4:26). He doesn't tell us not to get angry, but rather to give up our right to act out in anger in ways that are unhealthy, which is really all sin is—choices that are unhealthy for us and disconnect us from God and others.

Even when circumstances *were* my fault, I had to let go of my right to berate myself for hours on end and rip myself to shreds over it. I had to let go of my right to retreat emotionally and hide away from life. Very rarely do we make poor choices in an emotional vacuum. There is almost always pain behind the choice. That pain usually involves someone else. Being willing to get to the pain behind the choice, instead of exercising your right to ignore it, leads to emotional health.

Now ask yourself: What are some rights you may have to give up? It might be the right to lash out, or the right to shut down and emotionally retreat. It could be the right to hate someone, or the right to retaliate or manipulate. Remember as you explore this, God will never ask you to stuff your emotions away and pretend they're not there. Your emotions are what they are. Instead, you and I are exploring how we might *want* to choose to respond to our situation versus what's *best*. And what's best rarely involves actively expressing our negative rights. Proverbs 29:11 tells us, "A fool gives vent to his anger, but a wise man keeps himself under control."

If you come from a religious background be careful. Don't fall into the dangerous waters of knowing how you *should* feel so you never take the time to discover how you actually *do* feel. Resist the temptation of being the "good" girl or guy and get real. As you do, you will be able to be genuine with God, yourself and others, discover what rights you may need to let go of (including feeling justified), and allow God to truly begin to heal you.

When you think of some rights you need to let go of, what are some practical ways you can lean into God during the times you want to negatively let it all hang out? This is important. Just understanding that you shouldn't lash out or react poorly rarely helps. For me, I have to actively engage in the process of "how" with God. After all, He's the one who will provide me with the strength I need and the words I should use. And thank goodness! On my own I know I'm not strong enough to make the right choice. Even *with* God on my side I still blow it and sometimes make the wrong choices. Yet the more I wrestle through my situation with Him, the stronger my faith in His ability to rescue me grows. He helps me become better at fighting back.

Personally, I have read through many Psalms because it helped me remember that others have not only gone through challenging circumstances before me, but how I feel during those times isn't unique. I'm not alone, and God *is* there to guide me. I've learned to leave situations, if need be; to memorize scriptures that help me; to role play in my head or out loud the ways I could respond that honor the strength that God put within me and the respect He wants me to treat myself with, while deleting the ugly, unproductive gunk. Be sure to check out additional references at the end of the chapter for more resources to help you "get your brave on" and go deep. As Paul put it, "Finally, brothers and sisters, draw your strength and might from God" (Ephesians 6:10).

Remember: God's got your back. While you have a right to do whatever you want with your circumstances, you will find time and time again that when you give it to God, He's a lot more effective than you or I will ever be in handling it. Focus on what you *can* do with God, not at what you *can't* do on your own.

One important note to add is that surrendering your rights doesn't necessarily mean letting go of your legal rights to go after someone. If someone is a danger to others or to you, remember the arm of the law was given by God to protect you (see Romans 13:1-5). You may choose not to pursue someone legally as well. What matters in the process of deciding is protecting your own heart, thoughts and soul and seeking God's direction. Legal consequences can be the very best outcome in your situation, or may not be. Don't make that decision from a place of fear; decide based on where God is leading you, then trust the outcome.

FIGHTING THE LIES

Does this mean we're done? Not quite. Now that we've identified our fears, it's time to begin figuring out the lies we tell ourselves around those fears and what triggers them. Let's take a look at our list again. When I look at my mine—fear of succeeding and fear of the unknown—both are very different; yet they share a common root: I don't trust God. That is my deeper issue. Fear comes when I lack trust. As I learn my core issues and the deeper root behind them, I can begin finding scriptures to address the lies I tell myself when my fears get the best of me, and replace them with God's empowering truths. In short, I can begin to understand how to respond bravely to my situation.

In fact, being brave enough to face our lies and dismantle them one by one until we deeply believe God's truths for ourselves is key to emotional healing. Being one hundred percent honest with yourself and how you feel about it before God is crucial. It's hard to allow God to heal what you don't even see.

For me, my brave response has been to take the lies ("You're not worthy." "You will fail if you let go.") and replace them with truth ("I am worth *everything* to God, and He is completely trustworthy."). I look for practical ways to practice these truths in my day-to-day life. Sometimes it's giving myself a prayer "time-out." I need to either mentally or physically retreat for a brief moment or a few minutes to connect with my "dad" and let Him remind me of my worth and His strength. I've probably prayed from more bathroom stalls then I can mention doing just this. Sometimes it's to explore my thinking, to look at why I'm going to a place of fear to begin with. In doing so, I begin to understand my personal triggers.

Triggers are the deeper issues that bring your fears to the surface. In other words, what have you noticed that consistently sets you off? For me, financial stress was obviously a trigger. I tended to want to go to dark, scary places and react in dark, scary ways when I faced them. My triggers were very real. I had a bill due that I couldn't pay, or groceries to buy for my kids and no money to buy them with. I was working three jobs and going to graduate school during this time so I couldn't just work more. I was already maxed out.

To tackle this, I had to discover what my deeper issue was. After much prayer and thought, I began to realize I had a scarcity mindset stemming back to my childhood after my parent's divorce: "There's not going to be enough so I'd better do whatever I can do in the moment to get what I need." As I dug deeper with God, I began to see the root beneath the fear was trust. I didn't trust that God would meet my needs. There were many reasons I felt that way, all of which I spent time exploring with Him, but that was the bottom line.

Now when the triggers would come, instead of freaking out and melting into a paralyzed pile of emotion on the floor (okay, there was some of that, too!), I began praying that I would be able to trust in God to give me clarity, solutions, and sometimes even rescue. And God did. He showed up in the chunk of unexpected money I received with no strings attached the week I didn't have enough for gas, let alone groceries. He showed up in the people He put in my life to give me very specific direction on what to do and how to access resources available to help me.

Most importantly, He taught me how to relax in Him and know it was going to be okay regardless of outcome. Instead of feeling defeated and crushed during what was arguably the most challenging season of my adult life, I began to allow God to fight back for me. Instead of believing I was a failure and wallowing in anger, bitterness, and self-pity, kicking myself over bad decisions, I reminded myself again and again about God's vision and faith in me. I let him dismantle my faulty belief system and embrace His truth for me, knowing He is a God of abundance. And slowly but surely, with several steps forward and more than a few steps back, I emerged from the tunnel I was in, stronger and more confident in God's ability to provide for me and my ability to trust Him to do so. And He will do the same for you.

How about you? Is there a particular type of situation you always find difficult? Why? Maybe it's a negative relationship that needs some boundaries put in place. It might be times where you feel inadequate or insignificant, or when you allow something or someone to take you to a place where you feel less confident. Perhaps it's facing new situations or people. The more you understand your triggers, the more you can prepare for them in advance.

Prayerfully begin looking for what your triggers are. Begin to bravely explore new ways to fight against going to the dark places those triggers want to transport you to. Remember with God you *are* enough. Remember James 1:2-4:

> *Don't run from tests and hardships, brothers and sisters. As difficult as they are, you will ultimately find joy in them; if you embrace them, your faith will blossom under pressure and teach you true patience as you endure. And true patience brought on by endurance will equip you to complete the long journey and cross the finish line—mature, complete, and wanting nothing.*

I love the idea of being mature, of feeling complete. I especially like the idea of feeling like I'm wanting for nothing. I know it may feel a long way off right now, but this is what God desires for you. It begins by making a decision to honestly acknowledge your circumstances and feelings, to dig toward the root issues, looking for your triggers as you go, and realizing God wants to heal and help you, even in the moments you don't feel it.

FINAL BRAVE THOUGHTS

I can't end without letting you know one last important reality you will discover when you start getting your brave on. If you're working through a particularly long, difficult tunnel, it's important to know that when you quit running from your issues and actually start dealing with them, it can be a bit like opening Pandora's box. Remember Pandora? She's the mythological

Greek gal who was told not to open a box but was so curious to discover what was inside she opened it anyway—and all sorts of evils were released into the world. In other words, things got really bad for a time. Yet when she got to the bottom of the box, Pandora discovered an important weapon to combat all those evils: hope.

As you start working through what's blocking you, don't be surprised if sometimes it feels harder before it feels better. It doesn't mean you've taken a bad detour; it means you're one step closer to grabbing hold of genuine hope and vision for your life that waits for you at the end. Holding onto your vision as you work through such challenges is crucially important. It keeps you from losing heart. Sometimes we're like a baby who wants to stay in that dirty diaper—at least it's comfortable and we know and understand it. Give yourself permission to take breaks when you need them, but don't quit! You *will* get there. God has promised you, and He's true to his word.

Be sure to do things that nourish your spirit as you go through this life season. When dealing with all the challenges, it's easy to get lost in the struggle. Take time for yourself, however small. Get that manicure; take that walk; drive and listen to the station *you* like at the volume *you* prefer. Watch that movie you know you'll love. Take a nap. Get out in nature. Play that round of golf. Do whatever it is that makes your heart smile, and remind yourself of the many blessings you do have.

Paul tells us in Philippians 4:8:

> *Finally, believers, whatever is true, whatever is honorable and worthy of respect, whatever is right and confirmed by God's word, whatever is pure and wholesome, whatever is lovely and brings peace, whatever is admirable and of good repute; if there is any excellence, if there is anything worthy of praise, think continually on these things [center your mind on them, and implant them in your heart].*

You will have to look at a lot of ugly as you work through your tunnel, but don't forget to look for the good things all around you, too. Search for it if need be. And remember—God is holding your hand through the process. It is a roller coaster ride with many highs and lows. But with God, over time the ride evens out and you will disembark to continue forward on your life's journey.

SUMMARY

Day-to-day bravery is a process. It begins by engaging with God, embracing the messiness you find in your life, and learning to work through your tunnel with your Creator. It continues every time you remember to define yourself by God's view of who you are, not by your circumstances.

Hand over to Him what you have no control over, and face your fears. Surrender your rights to God. Discover the lies the enemy throws your way and what triggers them, then replace them with truth.

Yes, it takes bravery to face our mistakes and learn from them. It takes bravery to tackle situations we view as being other people's faults and to be willing to discover how we can grow even within that situation. Yet as we lean into God, our challenges and our victories will refine us into something greater. We become men and women of character, the battle-seasoned warriors who are wise and strong and free—true survivors. This is God's plan for us, His hope and desire for us. "Yes, be bold and strong! Banish fear and doubt! For remember, the Lord your God is with you wherever you go" (Joshua 1:9).

FOR FURTHER THOUGHT

1. Write down one of the major lies you tend to believe about yourself.

2. Write down one or two reasons why you may feel this way, and what one or two of your triggers may be.

3. When you buy into this lie, what happens?

4. How can you dismantle the faulty belief system?

5. How does God feel about you during this situation? Find a scripture that helps remind you of God's truth for you.

CHAPTER 5

STRENGTH FOR THE JOURNEY
Connection To Others

*"It makes me sad that so many people feel they're only allowed to show
their best face, while their humanity and vulnerabilities are forbidden and
hidden. How else do we connect, but by commonality, by mutual understanding
and truth in life's experiences? Whether it makes you smile or cringe, a truth
spoken is a healing thing."* — Jennifer DeLucy

You may wonder why there's a chapter on friendship in the middle of a
book about working through personal tunnels, especially since your tunnel
is just that—personal. It's easy, really. Friendship is an essential ingredient
in life. Whether you're an introvert or an extrovert, we are all wired to need
connection with others, and having that connection is one of the key ways
God helps us move through our tunnel more effectively.

Solomon, considered the wisest man of his generation, said, "By yourself
you are unprotected. With a friend you can face the worst. Can you round
up a third? A three-stranded rope isn't easily snapped" (Ecclesiastes 4:12).
Friends are the people who help strengthen you for the journey of life, and
the giving and receiving of true friendship is a delicate yet beautiful dance
that gives us purpose and meaning.

I've had periods in my life with very few deep friends and those times
were without a doubt some of the harder times emotionally for me. Interestingly, they weren't the times I've gone through the hardest circumstances;
sometimes my circumstances were just fine. But I felt alone on my journey
and isolated. The bone crushing, heart wrenching times in my life have been
brutal to be sure, but I have been blessed to have deep, close, honest relationships during most of those storms, and having them made those times much
more bearable.

God tells us, "A true friend loves regardless of the situation, and a real
brother exists to share the tough times" (Proverbs 17:17). So often, it has
been my close relationships that have helped me hear God's voice and have
encouraged me to make choices that pulled me away from adversity and
propelled me forward toward strength and freedom. I believe God gives us
friendships for that reason. Consider the following:

Wounds from a friend can be trusted. (Proverbs 27:6)

A man's counsel is sweet to his friend. (Proverbs 27:9)

A despondent person deserves kindness from his friend, even though he strays from the fear of the Highest One." (Job 6:14)

Friends come and friends go, but a true friend sticks by you like family. (Proverbs 18:24)

Love one another the way I loved you. This is the very best way to love. Put your life on the line for your friends. (John 15:11-13)

In the same way that iron sharpens iron, a person sharpens the character of his friend. (Proverbs 27:17)

These scriptures are a quick snapshot of what strong, healthy relationships should be. The hard things can be said because I know they come from a place of love and a genuine desire to help me be my best. Much needed comfort and encouragement are offered as I navigate through my tunnel. Sometimes that key person gives me a gentle push at just the right moment. Sometimes it's actually a much-needed shove. Either way, it's my key relationships that help me understand in a much deeper way God's love for me.

Friendship, in fact, is part of God's design to help us understand His love and grace for us—not just in the giving of friendship but in the receiving of friendship, too. In 1 John 4:12 we are told, "… if we love one another, God dwells deeply within us, and his love becomes complete in us—perfect love!" It is through the interconnectedness of relationship God makes us stronger, complete.

U2 front man Bono describes this idea when he shared his thoughts about being in a band versus being a solo artist several years ago. He believes solo artists are too prone to indulgence, and used his good friend Prince, now since passed, as an example:

I think, in some ways, it's easier to realize a vision that's singular and in your head, but it's harder to keep the vision going without argument. Look at Prince. He is one of my favorite composers of the twentieth century. I really believe in him. But he needs an editor. He needs a row. He needs somebody in the studio to tell him off: "And guess what? There's six great tracks and four of them are pretty average. I'm sorry, sir. Your genius was having a bad day." Does he have that? No chance.

Clearly, positive relationships push us to be better.

Yet the Bible also makes clear that not every friend is equal. Some friends come and go; some stay by our side no matter what happens. Some can be trusted; others can hurt you. Proverbs 12:26 puts it this way: "The righteous choose their friends carefully, but the way of the wicked leads them astray."

Good relationships involve *choice*.

There are many examples of positive friendships in the Bible and the world—Jonathon and David, Elijah and Elisha, Naomi and Ruth, Paul and Timothy to name a few. These were priceless relationships where each person helped the other to grow, strengthen and move forward in life powerfully. That said, there are also some negative examples of relationships in the Bible and the world—Cain and Abel, Samson and Delilah, Jezebel and Ahab, and even Barnabas and Paul. Some of these relationships were downright destructive. Each person spurred the other on toward evil, bitterness and heartache. In the case of Barnabas and Paul, they sharply disagreed on an issue and parted paths. Their friendship was deep and powerful for a season, but their journeys diverged and they went their separate ways.

One of the secrets to powerful growth is to choose your friends wisely, to be intentional about whom you pull into your life. Not all friends are created equal, and some friends who were perfect for one season in our life may not be the best fit for the season we currently find ourselves in. Just understanding those two statements puts great power at your fingertips—the power to choose people (yes, you get to choose) who actually help build you up, and the power to realize sometimes people are no longer the best companions to move forward with you on your journey. The first helps you to surround yourself with people who genuinely "get" you and have your best interests at heart. The second frees you from the guilt you can sometimes experience when a friend, despite your best efforts, no longer does get you and isn't going to necessarily help you make the best choices moving forward. It hurts, it's hard, but it's a normal part of the process.

WISE ADVISORS

The friends I have in my life—the ones I know are there for me through thick or thin, come hell or high water—I call my Wise Advisors. These are the friends who will tell me what I need to hear, not what I want to hear. Even if I don't listen, they still love me, accept me, and make me feel safe and secure in our friendship. They don't tell me, "I told you so." They don't judge me. They just love me and are committed to helping me on my journey, and I do the same for them. Okay, sometimes they tell me, "I told you so," but you get the idea!

Now I have several friends, as most of us do, and those friendships serve different roles in my life. Some are buddies I play sports with. Some are people who love books the way I do, and our friendship is built around that love. Some are people I've known all my life so they have a unique perspective of me, and I of them. I have colleagues, fellow church members, friends from small groups, from volunteering, etc. Yet it should be a very select few amongst all of these people who become Wise Advisors.

These are special relationships, intentional relationships. They're the relationships you work to cultivate and grow. Researcher and author Brené Brown puts it this way: "We cultivate love when we allow our most vulnerable and powerful selves to be deeply seen and known, and when we honor the spiritual connection that grows from that offering with trust, respect, kindness and affection. [It's] the energy that exists between people when they feel seen, heard, and valued; when they can give and receive without judgment; and when they derive sustenance and strength from the relationship." These are the people who accept your weaknesses and aren't intimidated by your strengths. These are the people who add deep value to your life, and you offer it to them in return.

Being our genuine selves means not just showing each other the pretty, polished parts, though that's important too. It means being willing to be vulnerable and messy with others, and to accept their messiness in return. Without vulnerability, we can't connect deeply. And without deep connection, we stunt our spiritual and emotional growth.

Research shows we heal and move forward most effectively when we allow our genuine selves to be seen. Study after study1 shows how going through adversity with Wise Advisors by our side helps us build resiliency, which is the ability to recover readily from illness, depression, adversity, and the like. Whether it's post-traumatic stress syndrome, deciding if the guy you're dating is "Mr. Right" or deciding on your next business move, having someone to talk to about your challenges in a genuine, real way *is* what allows us to feel seen, heard and valued. It offers us a sense of significance and peace.

And no, you don't have to be an extroverted social butterfly to develop strong emotional connections. You don't have to be a "people person." Remember it's not the quantity or even the length of time that counts in relationship; it's the quality. Personally, I have found introverts actually have some advantages over extroverts in developing deep relationships because they tend to have very rich mental lives. Since they are more inclined to think deeply about issues, they have some wonderful, profound wisdom to offer and tend to make thoughtful, caring friends. So, don't let your introverted nature be an excuse; let it be the asset God meant it to be. You and I *do* need close friends!

Muhammed Ali very famously said, "Friendship is the hardest thing in the world to explain. It's not something you learn in school. But if you haven't learned the meaning of friendship, you really haven't learned anything." Fortunately, God does teach us what it means to be a friend, and how to build strong ones at that. If not having Wise Advisors in your life is your personal tunnel, take heart. The best way to begin is by learning those godly characteristics and putting them into play in your own life. More than anything else, that will help you cultivate true, lasting friendships. Let's briefly touch on this.

CREATING RICH FRIENDSHIPS

As basic as it sounds, a great first step is defining for yourself what makes a good friend. Take out your iPad, laptop or an old-fashioned piece of paper and a pen and write down what qualities you would like to find in a Wise Advisor. These were some of mine:

- Unselfish
- Cares about my needs
- Not Reactionary
- Good Listener
- Assumes the best about me unless I show them otherwise
- Initiates
- Encouraging
- Giving
- Fun!

Next, step back and ask yourself how *you* do in each of these areas. Do you listen well, or do you have a tendency to think of your response while someone is talking, then interrupt so you can make your point? Do you react when people tell you messy truths about themselves by pulling back? Or feel the need to quickly jump in and fix someone versus helping them find their own answers? Start praying about who you are as a friend and put your vision and bravery into practice by slowly tackling these things.

Not sure what to put on your list? Start by reading scriptures about friendship and asking yourself what you need in relationship and how to carefully and judiciously begin offering those qualities to others. Refer back to Chapter Two for how to find scriptures if need be.

Jesus tells us, "Don't pick on people, jump on their failures, and criticize their faults— unless, of course, you want the same treatment. Don't condemn those who are down; that hardness can boomerang. Be easy on people; you'll find life a lot easier. Give away your life; you'll find life given back, but not merely given back—given back with bonus and blessing. Giving, not getting, is the way. Generosity begets generosity" (Luke 6:38). It's in the giving of ourselves as a quality friend that we are able to receive that quality in return.

You may be surprised to find you have more friends by your side simply by focusing on this. Either way, once we know how to be a friend we're in a much better position to find friends.

So now you're on board with the importance of maintaining strong, genuine relationships in your life, of finding your own Wise Advisor. How do we find these people? It's not like we can just put out a post saying, "Wanted: Wise Advisor to be Lifelong Friend." Well, we could but I'd be afraid of who might respond. No, the best way to begin, as with so many other things, is simply by praying. Begin to ask God to place people in your life you can really trust and confide in, people you can lean on.

After you've prayed, look up and look around. You may already have someone in your sphere you can connect with. It could be an acquaintance you've always admired, a relative you've always viewed as trustworthy, or someone you have felt drawn to. I know I did.

There was a lady I'd known for a few years as an acquaintance. She was on the outer ring of my friendships. I'd started to pray for more spiritual relationships when she and I independently decided to join a six-week Bible study. There were a lot of great women in this group, but there was something about her that drew me. I very purposefully asked her if she'd like to hang out sometime. I had no idea if she would end up being a great friend or not. There have been other people I've reached out to and nothing much really materialized from our time together. But this time, we just immediately connected.

At first, I was really there for her more than she was for me. While that's not a bad thing—being a Wise Advisor for someone else is a deep blessing—I really needed a more reciprocal relationship. Yet over time, our relationship became more and more mutual. As she grew spiritually, she was able to give more and more. Today she is by far one of my closest and dearest friends. I deeply value our relationship and know without a doubt she would do anything for me, just as I would do anything for her. I trust her advice and her wisdom. I accept her limitations and weaknesses just as she accepts mine. This couldn't have happened if I hadn't taken the time to get to know her, to feel out where she was at, and to be patient and let our friendship evolve over time.

Even if you look up and at first glance there's no one around, take heart. Keep praying and go searching. You might find someone in a support group, or while you're volunteering for something you feel passionate about. Join a bible study or small group at a local church; take a class that interests you at your local university. Join a sports league. Then carefully and intentionally reach out to people around you who feel drawn to. Ask them to lunch, to a movie, to grab a glass of wine after work—it doesn't really matter what, just try. Some may not be a fit; some may stay casual friends. Yet with prayer and purpose, you will be able to find someone you can really connect with.

We've spent some time discussing the importance of finding Wise Advisors in our lives and in understanding the important role that connection plays in helping us get through our tunnels. As we all know, however, there's no such thing as a perfect relationship. When two imperfect people come together there will be challenges. There is never an exception to this! As we work on developing deep, meaningful relationships that help us grow, let's tackle some of the cave-ins we encounter as we walk together toward the end of our tunnel.

USE DISCERNMENT

Probably the biggest challenge we face when we decide to be vulnerable is to let ourselves be "seen" versus letting ourselves get burned by others. We've all likely experienced a time where we let down our guard down with someone only to have them turn around and use that information against us, sometimes in some pretty brutal ways. As you build and invest in Wise Advisor relationships, it's important to make people earn the right to get to know the fantastic person you are. That's right—they need to earn it. And so do you.

In Matthew 10:16 Jesus is getting ready to send his followers out to help, and to connect with people. He gives them valuable advice: "Listen: I am sending you out to be sheep among wolves. You must be as shrewd as serpents and as innocent as doves." Now there are many ideas to be teased out of that statement, but for our purposes I'm going to focus in on just one—discernment. Discernment is the ability to step back and separate the forest from the trees. It means slowing down enough to objectively look at what is happening and base your decisions on fact, not emotion. Think of it as the actual truth in a situation.

You need to use discernment in your relationships. Discernment helps you decide who *does* earn that place of honor in your life since not everyone deserves a golden ticket into all that is you. Let people in by degrees as they've shown they can handle it. Proverbs 12:26 tells us, "A righteous man is cautious in friendship." Don't let emotion or need cloud your judgment. Be yourself always, but you don't always need to let all of yourself hang out.

When you do get burned, let it go. Better to err on the side of love than the side of hate. And remember that modern day piece of wisdom from Oprah Winfrey: "When someone shows you who they are, believe them." If you are the one making all the effort all the time, if confidences aren't honored and reciprocated, no matter how great the person seemed initially, he or she is not the one for you. Always place actions over words. Always.

As hard as it is to face, some friends—maybe even some current ones—are not out for your good. These are the folks you need to allow God to prune out of your life. Jesus tells us, "I am the Real Vine and my Father is the Farmer. He cuts off every branch of me that doesn't bear grapes. And every branch that is grape-bearing he prunes back so it will bear even more fruit" (John 15:1-2). You don't have to be a gardener to get the idea. There are times when something in our lives needs to be removed in order to make way for something even better. This extends to people.

Unfortunately, some friendships are downright toxic. Without a doubt, these are the relationships you need to allow God to prune from your life. Do you have a friend who is your partner in crime, your "sin buddy?" I definitely have! These are the people I picked purely because I knew they would let me do what I wanted, how I wanted, to whom I wanted, regardless of how negative the outcome might be. If I wanted to do drugs, they were right there offering them to me. If I wanted to have sex with someone, they were encouraging me to exercise my sexual freedom. If I wanted to be a cold-hearted bitch to someone, they agreed I should. I'm sure you can read between the lines and realize I did the same for them. These are not the healthy relationships we need. If you're in these types of relationships, you need to allow them to be pruned from your life so you can make way for something better.

GET YOURSELF OUT OF THE WAY

Another cave-in that can derail our relationships is much harder to see: ourselves. Pruning isn't just about removing the weak branches next to you. It's also about removing your own. All of us have hidden character flaws—hidden from us, that is. Usually those around us are well aware of them, but we can't see them—yet another reason we need close friends to give us truth. Since they aren't things that we're readily aware of, it's harder for us to allow them to be pruned. Learning to open yourself up to have the delicate, tender areas of your life, the hidden, vulnerable spaces, will by far bring the greatest abundance.

When it comes to relationships, if you're consistently finding yourself in conflict with people, if you always seem to have recurring, ongoing issues, there comes a point in time where you have to ask yourself an uncomfortable question: Are you the common denominator? This can be scary, since negative behavior almost always stems from a dark place within us. Yet if there was ever a time to get your brave on, it's here.

If you find yourself always assuming the worst of people and their motives, if you're quick to come to judgment against others, or if you constantly struggle with feeling inferior and less, you have a strong probability of being the person who is most in need of change in your friendships. If you catch yourself just looking for people to agree with your opinions instead of being willing to receive contradictory opinions with an open mind and heart, again you may be the issue. If you start pulling back from people the moment you begin to connect with them, coming up with flimsy reason why they aren't good for you, it's time to take a hard look within.

In these moments of self-exposure, take heart! Once again, you're going to find you're in good company. The Apostle Peter is someone I think most of us would say was a pretty rocking guy. I mean, the man penned books that made it into the Bible. He was one of Jesus' closest friends. Not too shabby. Yet when Jesus most needed him, Peter wasn't there. He was falling asleep. He was thinking about saving his own skin. He was consumed with worry about how other people might perceive him (read the last two chapters of John for an up close and personal view). Because of it, he ended up denying Jesus not once, not twice, but three times. Not exactly Peter's finest moment.

Yet one thing Peter did do—when he realized his error, he got his brave on and he faced up to it. Peter could've blamed Jesus for not being the kind of Messiah he thought Jesus should be. He could've felt sorry for himself and felt like no one understood the pressures he faced as Jesus' right-hand guy. Instead, he chose to wrestle through his fear, insecurity, self-focus and, yes, his shame, before he arrived at a place where he was ready to connect with Jesus again. Yet once he did reconnect, wow! He went on to lead the early church from a small group of believers to a worldwide movement. Not bad for a sometimes self-absorbed fisherman.

So, don't be afraid to face yourself. Ask people for one area they see in which you most need to grow as a friend, and then be willing to receive their answers without justifying, making excuses or getting angry. Ask them also for the things you're doing right. It always helps to remember the good, too.

BE OPEN TO RECEIVE

As you learn to become a good friend to others, remember to allow others to be a good friend to you. When you're going through a tough situation, you need to allow others to help you. I'll be honest. Letting others help me in tangible ways was probably the hardest lesson I learned as God led me through my tunnel. You see, I loved to help other people. But I was tremendously uncomfortable with letting others help me.

God eventually had to allow me to be backed into a corner where I had no choice but to ask for help. I'll never forget the moment. During that season in my life, I had a small but mighty group of Wise Advisors that I would collectively reach out to for extra prayer. I was looking at the end of a month where no child support had come in, and despite the three jobs I was working, there wasn't enough left over to buy gas so I could even *get* to work to try and make more money. In the meanwhile, I had three kiddos looking to me to feed them and meet their emotional needs as they were going through their own tunnels at the same time. Talk about stressful.

I will never forget that moment of desperation, of how it felt to literally have no answer, no solution, just cold fear gripping at my heart and mind. Since I had no solution, I emailed my Wise Advisors for prayer. Let me tell you I would have *never* sent an email explaining such personal financial challenges had I not been in such desperate need of God to show me a solution. What happened next still makes me tear up when I think about it.

The husband of one of my friends showed up at my door that night, envelope in hand. He just smiled and handed it to me and said it was a small gift. Then before I could so much as blink, he left. When I opened the envelope, there was a large sum of money—enough to get me through the rest of the month. I just cried. It was humbling; it was amazing; it blew me away to have someone do something like that for me.

Of course, I immediately called my friend to thank her. Though I offered to pay her back someday, she made it very clear it was a gift. She then let me know someone had done the very same thing for them once when they had been in a very tight situation. When they had asked if they could pay back such generosity, all they were told to do was pay it forward. I could hear in her voice she was tearing up, too, as she shared, "Now we're in a situation where we can finally pay it forward. Praise God! And that's all I would ask of you. Pay it forward someday."

Listen again to what was going on in that conversation. Had I stuck to my stubborn pride and not allowed her to help me (which I normally would've done), not only would I not have received rescue, but I would have kept her from giving a back a blessing she had long been waiting to give. When you allow others to serve you, blessings flow all around. Whether it's money or help around the house or meals or whatever, allowing people to help you in tangible ways during times of struggle is a powerful thing.

Proverbs 17:19 puts it this way: "Whoever builds a high gate invites destruction." When you refuse to let others inside your situation, ultimately you pay the price. You may make it through on your own, but you will lose out on the many amazing benefits that come from letting people come along side you and help.

THE ROLE OF ADVICE

No conversation about connecting with the Wise Advisors in your life would be complete without discussing the role of advice in friendship. The whole idea of a Wise Advisor is actually pulled from a scripture that says, "Refuse good advice and watch your plans fail; take good counsel and watch them succeed" (Proverbs 15:22). The point is obvious: We are collectively much better when we get solid advice about our lives versus going out and just doing what seems best to us.

Notice there are some important qualifiers in the scripture. Good advice and good counsel have one word in common: "good." Finding good advice is not about running around trying to grab advice from anyone who will listen. It's also not about getting advice from the people you know who will "bolster your case." With effort, you know you can find *someone* who will agree with you and tell you what you want to hear regardless of how "good" what you're looking to do is or isn't. At the end of the day, it won't bolster you; it will bust you.

I know for me there are times I do this with God. I don't like the answer I sense He's giving me. So rather than wrestling through that feeling and listening, I start to let the creator of doubts in. *You probably didn't hear that right,* I'll think. *Maybe you should talk to a few other people just to be sure.*

Ha! It's not that I'm unsure. It's that I don't like the answer. And somehow, I always seem to know one person who, if I position the information just right, will tell me what I want to hear so I can feel more justified in doing what I want. But that's Satan. He loves to jump in my head and twist things. It always comes back to bite me in the end.

Of course, it only takes getting knocked around good and hard a few times in my tunnel to realize the only person I'm fooling by running after that sort of advice is myself. God is patient. He'll let me knock myself out a few times if need be until I learn the lesson, and seeking good advice is no exception.

I have learned the first step to finding quality advice starts with prayer. Meeting with your Creator first before you meet with anyone else, even if briefly, invites His wisdom into your situation. Asking God for direction, and for a willing spirit to receive direction, help you get your heart centered for the answers. God is never stingy with giving you wisdom. Quite the opposite. The book of James tells us, "If you don't have all the wisdom needed for this journey, then all you have to do is ask God for it; and God will grant all that you need. He gives lavishly and never scolds you for asking" (James 5). Let Him lavish you.

The other benefit of praying first is that it invites God in to line up the people you need. While oftentimes it's your Wise Advisors that become your go-to people, they may not always have a piece of the puzzle you require. I am continually amazed at how God has placed someone new in front of me at exactly the right time that has the knowledge, wisdom or connection I need. It's almost eerie. Yet I believe it comes from God granting me all I need because I took the time to ask.

Okay. You've prayed and gotten yourself centered in order to receive challenges and advice from the people you trust to be honest with you. After you've explained, listen. Let me say it again: Listen! James 1:19 tells us, "Listen, open your ears, harness your desire to speak, and don't get worked up into a rage so easily." Ask clarifying questions if need be, but make it safe for someone to be honest with you. Don't squash what is being said or shut down the conversation verbally or nonverbally with your response.

Then take what is true to heart. Not everything everyone has shared with me has been accurate, but there's usually some truth lurking around in there. I think of my heart as the bull's eye of a target with rings spreading out. If someone shoots an arrow with the goal of reaching my heart, not to hurt me but to help me grow, the arrow may miss center. Maybe sixty percent of what is shared is accurate and applies. I don't have to own the forty percent that doesn't fit, but I miss out on so much when I choose to only focus on what is *wrong* with what's being said, instead of homing in on what is *right*. That sixty percent could change my life. If my shoulder is hit instead of my heart, I have to grab hold of my bravery and take the arrow from my shoulder and put it into my heart myself.

Proverbs 24:3-4 tells us, "By wisdom a house is built, and through understanding it is established; through knowledge its rooms are filled with rare and beautiful treasures." We are God's temple, His "house." When we have enough wisdom to listen to what is being said and seek to understand how it applies to us, rare and beautiful gifts fill our hearts and lives in every sense. My Wise Advisors have been such a huge part of the mistakes I've been able to avoid, the successes I've been able to have, the healing I've been able to receive and the rich growth I've experienced in my life. They have lavishly blessed me!

At the end of the day, however, the voice we must always listen to and follow most closely is God's. There are several examples in the Bible of people who were called by God to do something even though everyone else around them didn't agree or thought of them as crazy. Think of Noah building his ark, or Paul setting off to Rome at the end of his life. Everyone else said don't. God said do. Let God win that argument. Last time I checked, He's the one who most knows what He's doing.

This principle doesn't apply to character issues. If everyone who knows me well tells me I have a selfish streak, but I feel like God is telling me I don't, guess what: I'm selfish. Proverbs 26:28 tells us, "A lying tongue hates those it hurts, and a flattering mouth works ruin." Never forget those lies and that flattery can come from within you.

EXTEND GRACE

Remember, too, people will disappoint you, just as you will disappoint others. Cut your Wise Advisors slack, just as God cuts you slack. No one is a perfect friend, not even you. Jesus was, of course, a perfect friend, but his buddies still let Him down big time. When he most needed them in the Garden of Gethsemane the night before his execution, they kept falling asleep. Jesus challenged Peter, "Could you men not keep watch with me for one hour?" But He continues with, "Watch and pray so that you will not fall into temptation. The spirit is willing, but the body is weak" (Matthew 26:40-41).

Jesus knew the hearts of his friends. He knew they loved Him and that in their spirits they were committed to Him. Yet their flesh, their follow through if you will, could be weak sometimes. Jesus didn't just say, "Well, these guys don't get me," abandon them and scrap the whole thing. He directed them back to prayer and to God. He was patient and gracious. We do well when we do the same.

Make sure you have realistic expectations for your friendships. I have met people who demand so much from others they are set up for failure. The time, the effort, the needs they expect someone else to meet are so great, their friendships crush beneath the weight. Remember—a Wise Advisor does not replace God. That empty hole in our hearts can only be filled by Jesus dwelling within us. No one else can "complete" you or make you happy. Only God can do that. Don't ask people, through your expectations, to take on God's role in your life. It hurts them and it hurts you.

Usually, those of us who tend to get hurt in friendships get hurt because we are "givers" by nature. We love to give to the people we care about, to help others out, to be a lavish friend. Where we can get into trouble is when we do this chiefly because we want that same generous attention in return. Then, when we don't receive back what we perceive as our due, we pull the plug on the whole relationship, or drastically pull back, often because of one statement or one action, leaving the other person bewildered and confused. They haven't been keeping a running tally of all of your "good deeds" the way you have. Which is sort of the point of friendship. We give because we choose to give, the way Jesus did, with no expectation. Be realistic in what you expect out of your friendships. That person is not your god. And you shouldn't become theirs.

MAINTAIN HEALTHY BOUNDARIES

Which leads to the final point. Even the best of relationships need healthy boundaries in place. A boundary is a limit or a line you place between you and someone else. When you let someone in by degrees, you are intentionally drawing a more generous boundary line, giving that person access into the special areas of your life *as it has been earned.* Cutting out a destructive relationship from your life is a decision to draw a line between you and someone else, no longer allowing that person full access (or any access) to all that is you.

We've talked about forgiveness, about grace and extending mercy to others. We've talked about fighting to maintain relationships that are worth fighting for. But we still need healthy boundaries in place, boundaries that acknowledge our worth before God (i.e. abusive or destructive language and actions toward me or those I love aren't acceptable…); boundaries that keep us spiritually and emotionally healthy (…therefore you will have more limited or no access to me and/or those I love).

You draw a healthy boundary when you set realistic expectations for your relationships that say, "I understand you won't be perfect. I won't be, either. Let's do our best to support and encourage one another in Christ as we move forward, extending grace to each other and with necessary time apart if need be so we stay healthy in our friendship." We will talk about this more later, but for now, remember that healthy Wise Advisor relationships are safe relationships with healthy, realistic boundaries in place to protect you both.

If Jesus is the wind that fills my sails, it is my Wise Advisors who help me watch my compass so I don't go off course. They remind me to go where the wind takes me, whether light or strong. They help me remember the journey is worth taking, and the destination we're headed for is glorious. We laugh together, cry together, share our stories and our scars, our joys and our fears. And our journeys are the richer for it.

As you work through your tunnel, whatever it may be, pull in your Wise

Advisors. Lean on them, just as you would want them to be able to lean on you. Let them help; let them be present. "Just as lotions and fragrance give sensual delight, a sweet friendship refreshes the soul" (Proverbs 27:9). Let your soul be refreshed.

SUMMARY

We are wired to need relationships, but not all relationships are created equally. Some relationships, in fact, are toxic and need to be cut out of our lives. Yet we all need Wise Advisors, people who have our best interests at heart and are committed to helping us grow. You can tell if someone is a Wise Advisor if they are willing to tell you the truth even if it's painful, and they are willing to love you in the midst of your messiness. These are intentional relationships that need to be nourished and developed, partly by being a strong friend in return. Wise Advisors are great resources for prayer, advice and support, and they will help refresh your spirit.

FOR FURTHER THOUGHT

1. Take time to evaluate your friendship skills. What are you strong in? What areas need attention so you can grow?
2. In Luke 6:38 it says: "Don't hold back—give freely, and you'll have plenty poured back into your lap—a good measure, pressed down, shaken together, brimming over. You'll receive in the same measure you give." How does this apply to your current friendships?
3. Come up with one specific action you can take this week to grow as a friend.

REFERENCES

Bonanno, G. (2010). *The Other Side of Sadness: What the new Science of Bereavement Tells Us About Life After Loss*. New York, NY: Basic Books.

Brown, B. (2012). *Daring Greatly*. New York, NY: Gotham Books.

Brown, B. (2010). *The Gifts of Imperfection: Let Go of Who You think You're Supposed to Be and Embrace Who You Are*. Center City, MN: Hazelden Publishing.

Lind, K. (2015). *Time to Get Vulnerable: Why the Best Leaders View Vulnerability as a Strength*. Retrieved from http://www.watercoolernewsletter. com.

Moore, B. (2008). *Looking Up When Life is Looking Down*. Nashville,

TN: Thomas Nelson.

    Young, K. (2015, April 10). *Vulnerability: The Key to Close Relationships.* Retrieved from http://www.heysigmund.com.

CHAPTER 6

START DIGGING
Intentionality

"Times of transition are strenuous, but I love them. They are an opportunity to purge, rethink priorities, and be intentional about new habits. We can make our new normal any way we want." — Kristin Armstrong

I love the outdoors. When I lived in Flagstaff, Arizona, there was a National Park trailhead not more than 30 seconds away from my home. I could hike to my heart's content, inhaling the woodsy fresh scent of the Ponderosa pines, their fallen needles cushioning my every step as I explored the beauty around me. The night sky was so clean and clear, I could see the milky way galaxy just walking out into my backyard. If I took even a few minutes of time, I could easily find a falling star to wish upon. It was, in a word, gorgeous.

I have also lived in places that were anything but gorgeous. There was no innate beauty around me to admire, no nearby natural escapes to wander through. The main parts of town looked unkempt and forlorn. The landscape was monotonous, boring.

I have found life can be much the same way. What God wants for each one of us is a beautiful, amazing journey along a pathway specifically designed for us. Yet all too often, we get so busy making *our* plans, setting *our* goals and striving for some future date or situation, that we miss the daily choices and decisions God lays before us that allow our forward movement toward that beautiful, rich path. Our life begins to feel like drudgery because we keep treading the same old rutted, well-worn road we understand but don't deeply enjoy. We know we want better, but we don't stop long enough to listen each and every day for the ways the Lord is trying to direct us to the bountiful journey He has marked out for each of us.

Intentionality is all about making plans *with* God instead of making plans and hoping God will somehow come along for the ride. Do you know how long some researchers say the average New Year's resolution lasts? Thirty-six hours. That's it! Without true motivation that comes from developing a vision with and connection to God, our intentions fall by the wayside.

Before we jump into the nuts and bolts of being intentional, I think it bears value to briefly discuss what intentionality *is not*. It's not you running around doing whatever you think is the quickest, best solution to your given situation. It's not coming up with a laundry list of items that you find yourself buried under. And it's especially not you taking control of your situation.

A few things happen when we do that. Change can feel scary. When you default to doing what you understand (which brings comfort since you understand it), you're less likely to find a different outcome. It's doing the same thing over and over again but expecting a different result. It's frustrating. It's defeating. It doesn't move you forward. If we make a huge list of all that needs to change, we get overwhelmed. We begin to close our eyes and wish for escape; we paralyze ourselves and then we can't move forward.

When you take control of the situation—using your solution instead of falling to your knees, crying out and waiting for God's solution—you settle for less. Your solution may actually work, but it will never be as powerful as God's solution for you. It will never move you as far forward as God can. Plus, your solution requires you to have the strength and will to change yourself. Personally, I don't ever seem to have enough internal juice to do so. Being intentional with God allows us to tie in to His strength and will, which is infinite and mighty. His solution is one that lasts, one that will transform us and remove us from our pile of rubble.

WHAT IT MEANS TO BE INTENTIONAL

For those who are learning to tackle your challenges with faith, think of intentionality as the actual steps you take to exit your tunnel and enter into God's wonderful light. It's finding specific actions in order to move forward again with God's strength. This is where you come up with a specific plan.

As awesome as that sounds, being intentional can be hard to learn because we tend to want results right away, and when we don't get them it's easy to give up and quit. Intentionality requires motivation, and motivation can be hard to come by when you're living through a time of deep struggle and doubt. These are the times our failures like to parade themselves in front of us, trying to tell us we can't really change.

As a reminder, keep going back to finding your vision and connection with God and others as you work on being intentional. Remember to grab hold of your Moses-type bravery during your moments of doubt and distrust. Most importantly, remember to give yourself grace—just as God does.

Intentionality in itself is discovering through prayer and reflection with God what steps you need to take and how you will need to take them. It's more than making plans; it's making God central to your plan making. Like every other quality we've explored, intentionality is a process that grows and evolves with you over time as God directs your steps.

There are two different pieces to intentionality: addressing both your internal and external struggles. Usually the two go hand-in-hand. External struggles are the things going on outside of us—the bills that can't be paid, the boss who is overbearing, the drink in your hand, or losing someone you love. Think of external struggles as your outward circumstances. Internal struggles involve what's going on within us—depression, loneliness, self-loathing, fear or isolation. These are the emotions we feel on the inside. Almost always, the external is tied to the internal. In other words, your boss is a jerk (external) and you're angry and hurt by it (internal).

Bravery helps us tackle the internal pieces by finding our lies and replacing them with our spiritual truths. Notice that tackling the internal comes before tackling the external. That's because changed external behavior is ultimately tied to the heart. If you only deal with the circumstances without digging into the whys behind it, you are more apt to fall back to the old behavior. There's a scripture that puts it pretty bluntly: "As a dog returns to its vomit, so a fool repeats his foolishness" (Proverbs 26:11). Gross but true. I don't know about you, but that's not how I want my life to go. Psalm 28:7 tells us, "The Lord is my strength and my shield; my heart trusts in him, and he helps me." Notice the strength comes from a heart that's surrendered to and trusts in God, and so God helps him. It's the same with us.

Being intentional is a mindset and a process. It requires thoughtfulness and prayer. As you look at your tunnel, you gain an initial vision for where God wants to guide you. You connect with Him in order to receive that guidance, and the strength and encouragement you need for the journey. You share your vision with your Wise Advisors so they can pray for you, give you counsel, and hold you accountable if necessary. Then, you begin to bravely dismantle the internal lies and barriers that keep you trapped. As you do so, you prayerfully create specific, intentional actions that help you move forward. Each of these steps is wrapped up in intentionality. In other words, simply using this process *is* being intentional.

Remember 2 Corinthians 10:3-6:

The world is unprincipled. It's dog-eat-dog out there! The world doesn't fight fair. But we don't live or fight our battles that way—never have and never will. The tools of our trade aren't for marketing or manipulation, but they are for demolishing that entire massively corrupt culture. We use our powerful God-tools for smashing warped philosophies, tearing down barriers erected against the truth of God, fitting every loose thought and emotion and impulse into the structure of life shaped by Christ. Our tools are ready at hand for clearing the ground of every obstruction and building lives of obedience into maturity.

Intentionality is all about doing just that—using God's divine Spirit that He has placed in each and every one of us to free us from the yoke of slavery the world would put on us, and to liberate our hearts and minds for something far greater than we could ever obtain or become on our own.

INTENTIONALITY IN ACTION: CHALLENGE #1

Probably the best way to understand intentionality is to see it in action. Let's look together at an example to approach with intentionality: money issues. While this may not be your issue, role-playing through it will help you tackle your own.

In our money scenario, you have the external challenge of not having enough money each month to live on. This may stem from spending without a plan, or from spending recklessly, or from simply not making enough at work even though you're following your budget faithfully. Now within that challenge, you may face a whole host of internal struggles. You may be fearful of actually having a budget; maybe you associate it with being confined or with being poor. You may try to spend your way to happiness for that short-term pleasurable rush you get after the purchase. Or you may believe it's impossible for you to get better employment because you're not smart enough or you don't have enough time, or because you feel unsupported by those around you.

Being brave and intentional in this situation starts by identifying what the true issue is, both internally and externally. Let's say your challenge is a combination of all three spending issues: You don't have a real, working budget because it feels tiresome, you tend to spend what you know you don't have to make yourself feel better, and you know you're underemployed but you feel helpless to change it.

First, define what your goal is. The goal in this situation is pretty obvious. You want to have enough money left at the end of each month to do things like save, and to be able to retire someday. Simplify your goal to a short phrase: "Extra money each month." Begin praying for that specific goal each and every day, asking for God's guidance.

Now it's time to look at how to prayerfully achieve your goal. Recall that you have three separate challenges here—no budget, overspending and underemployment. The temptation would be to start tackling all three at once. Don't! Doing so will only overwhelm you and set you up for failure. You didn't get into this situation overnight and you won't get out of it overnight, either. Be thoughtful and intentionally pick one to start with.

Let's say you've landed on how to actually have a workable budget. You've decided that having more money but not knowing how to protect and take care of it would be counterproductive, and as you've prayed about it you sense God confirming your choice. Even if this is not your struggle, take a moment now and think of specific, smaller steps that will move you closer to understanding and maintaining a budget.

What did you come up with? Maybe you decided to get a book at the public library and work through it. Maybe you chose to sign up for a money management class you've heard they offer in your community or at church. Whatever you chose, what are the most basic steps? Write them down.

Let's say I've decided to tackle my budget challenge with a book. My basic steps might look something like this:

1. Use the internet to research budgeting books with high ratings for ease of use and understanding.
2. Reserve a copy at the local library or do an interlibrary loan.
3. Share my plan with my Wise Advisor(s), asking not only for prayer but for accountability with my follow-through.
4. Take a look at the content of the book and break it down into manageable sections, deciding what I'm going to read and when.
5. Create a list of tasks I will need to implement in order to maintain a healthy budget, thinking through each specific task and how I can do it each day, week, month, year, and so on.
6. Share my lessons and my progress with my Wise Advisor(s) as I work through the process.
7. Copy any worksheets or duplicate any formats I found particularly useful before I return the book.

The temptation in this scenario is to simply say, "I'll just grab a book and read it. Easy enough." It doesn't actually take a whole lot more time to write down a process and pray about it, but doing so will make a huge difference in actually following through with your plan. God reminds us in Proverbs 21:5, "Careful planning puts you ahead in the long run; hurry and scurry puts you further behind." Intentionality is all about slowing down enough to make thoughtful, prayerful choices instead of aimlessly running ahead. Always take the time to break down your goal into manageable steps, even if it seems relatively simple. Again, Proverbs tells us, "Know where you are headed, and you will stay on solid ground" (4:26).

Note that my list included my Wise Advisors. Inviting others into your process is so crucial. Asking for accountability helps keep you on task since you know someone is going to check in with you about it. And remember to choose people who are able to actually help you. In this scenario, I would want to pick someone who *is* strong financially, or who will at least value the process I'm undertaking. They will offer the best support. If you have a harder time breaking bigger goals down into smaller, manageable steps, your Wise Advisor(s) can also be a sounding board to help you with your process.

Remember that while the outcome may be to have more money each month, the process itself usually starts with one small step. After you take that one step, you then move on to take another, then another. As you gain a little growth with God and experience success, your strength begins to grow and so does your faith that with God you can tackle this. This is, in fact, the biggest difference from simply making yet another list versus prayerfully coming up with intentional solutions. Solutions are thoughtful, thorough, and typically require vision over time. You may accomplish one aspect of the task quickly, but it will take time to get to the outcome.

The other important piece of my budgeting puzzle will be to take time with God to figure out why I have such a hard time keeping a budget to begin with. It could be my parents argued about money all the time, so I associate any discussion about money with bad things. Or maybe it's because I don't feel worthwhile and the pleasure I receive from a purchase temporarily eases my pain, so I fear having that exposed on paper. If a budget seems boring and of little value to me, why is that? It may not be my natural strength, but I am aware there are benefits to having one, so why do I resist?

Regardless, I would take the time to really study out what God has to say about my lies and memorize scriptures that help me remember His truths for me, as we discussed in Bravery. Whenever my negative thinking gets the best of me, I'll bring them out so I can fight back with truth. You and I will have setbacks. The key is to keep your plan in front of you and to prayerfully keep returning to it.

CHALLENGE #2

As I work through my list and get some success with budgeting under my belt, I will prayerfully decide which issue to tackle next. Let's say I'm being nudged to begin focusing on the fact I'm underemployed. It doesn't matter how careful I am. In working my budget, I'm realizing that on my current income, I will be stuck living from paycheck to paycheck with no breathing room if I don't make some changes. Since this is a circumstance I have faced, I will share from my personal experience. Again, I need to explore both my external and internal circumstances.

For me, my external circumstances showed I wasn't making enough at the three jobs I was working to make ends meet. As a single parent with kids who were going through a lot emotionally, I didn't want to take on a fourth job and not be present for them, so my available time had some limitations. Well—and so did my stamina! I needed to get to a place where my financial livelihood was no longer dependent on what anyone else did or didn't do to help support my kids.

Internally, I had to work through deep fear that I couldn't do what needed to be done to financially support my children on my own. I had a lot of anger and resentment I had to work through for being thrust into this situation to begin with. I also felt overwhelmed a lot and hopeless, like the process would take too long and I would never get to a different space. After all, the bills were right in front of me. My creditors weren't waiting.

In complex situations such as this, I have found I use multiple lists over time. Some are written and some are mental notes depending on their importance. As I progress forward, my list will change and evolve with me. The whole point of being intentional is to make sure I'm not missing any angles so I have a greater chance of success. That's why constantly breaking your challenges down to their smallest components is so valuable.

I have also found it's during such difficult, complex challenges that my need to stay tied into God and His vision for me is non-negotiable. In other words, I'm in a longer battle and my answers won't come quickly. I will need every ounce of encouragement and strength God can give me to get through. While we will delve into this more deeply in Consistency, it's important to understand this is key to achieving your external goals.

So, with my underemployment situation, I started out by making a note of my priorities. I landed on these priorities after thoughtful prayer and discussion with my Wise Advisors on what I most needed. I also looked at what my priorities would be through the lens of honoring my God-given values. Since my family was my number one God-given priority, the other priorities I landed on had to honor that truth. Any solution that took me away from that was not going to be a God-honoring solution. Here's what I came up with:

PRIORITIES

1. Find a job that is flexible enough to allow time with my kids.
2. Find something that doesn't require lots of upfront training.
3. Find financial solutions for the interim period when my new job hasn't started yet and I'm still in my current challenge.

Once I landed on these priorities, each one was broken down into a detailed yet manageable step-by-step list. Each one required some research on my part. Each one required time and focus, just as the budgeting example did. Yet one by one I was able to knock off my list. I was able to finish my master's degree at a local university in a time frame that worked. I figured out what programs were available to me within my community for short-term help financially. I started exercising consistently to help cope with the stress. In short, I started being proactive instead of reactive. I quit being a victim of my circumstances and pain, and started allowing God and my Wise Advisors to guide me forward.

Through it all, I allowed myself to hurt, to get out what was going on internally through the process. I didn't find steps and solutions in a vacuum. There were many tears shed, many nights of wrestling with my fears and doubts. There were times that the light at the end of my tunnel seemed like a distant pinpoint, far from my reach. I was honest with God about my struggles, and turned often to His truths and vision for me so He could see me through. With prayer and thought, I found solutions, both inside and out.

Something you might notice about my goals: Some were immediate (what will I do for money now?), and some were more long term (finding a career that would work for me). Proverb 14:15 tells us, "The prudent give thought to their steps." Prudent just means to use wise judgment. Asking, "What do I need to do in the short term? What do I need to do in the long term?" helps you to do just that. Thoughtful steps also imply a process of moving forward. Having a nebulous plan with no idea of how to get there isn't really a plan. It's a dream. I have met many people who want something different in their lives, and sometimes it can even be something very specific; but they have no concrete, intentional plans that they're praying about. There is nothing they have allowed God to put into place, to get to where God is calling them to go. Remember: Vision involves action. Considering your steps is crucial, but then you must put them into place.

CHALLENGE #3

Finally, as I experienced success and growth in the area of underemployment, the last step in our illustration would be to tackle overspending. While this wasn't my particular issue, if it were I would take a close, hard look at my external and internal struggles. In our illustration, the external is buying things I don't truly need or really can't afford. The internal struggle is taking a hard, close look at *why* I'm trying to find my sense of self from a purchase. Stop and think for a moment—if this was your tunnel, why might you be buying when you shouldn't? What is broken inside that needs God's divine healing?

You may have come up with seeing yourself as less. You need that big, shiny truck to look manly and important because inside, if you're really honest, you feel like maybe you're not. Or you want the car because you feel you deserve it; you don't trust God or others to honor and bless you. Maybe it has been your life goal to own that truck, yet it doesn't align with God's life goals for you. Maybe you love the rush of pleasure you feel when you finally drive away with the truck; but you're not happy in general so you need the purchases to feel better about yourself. These issues may stem back to roots that run very deep, or they may arise from a current situation that has you doubting yourself. Either way, you need to bravely tackle the roots that lie beneath the surface.

If you've decided you're not very happy, for whatever reason, you will begin exploring that tunnel. With God at your side, ask yourself a lot of questions and prayerfully search until you find the answers. Bravely ask your Wise Advisors about what they might see going on in your heart and life as it relates to this issue. You may even seek professional help.

Let's say you realize the very root of your issue is you don't feel like you're really important or that you really matter to anyone, like your life has been one big letdown after another. Perhaps your parents never really nurtured you and you've never really worked through that; or perhaps you're in a relationship where you're trying to define your worth from how that individual sees you instead of defining yourself in God's eyes. Once you have a grasp of what's going on at the core, you can use God's word to find your spiritual truths. Ephesians 6:17 tells us God's word is like a sword in our hands, able to defend us against spiritual attack. And Hebrews 4:12 tells us, "His powerful Word is sharp as a surgeon's scalpel, cutting through everything, whether doubt or defense, laying us open to listen and obey. Nothing and no one is impervious to God's Word. We can't get away from it—no matter what." Hold the scriptures you connect with close to your heart.

You can then bravely explore what your triggers are, what situations, words or people have the ability to magically transport you to bad places seemingly against your will. Identifying these triggers enables you to put an action plan in place to help in those moments of weakness (we will discuss this more in Consistency). You will pull in your Wise Advisor(s) and find ways to hold yourself accountable for your spending, and have a safe place to go to for encouragement, challenge, comfort and/or a reminder of God's grace when one of your triggers fires.

As you create your action plan, you will pray a lot with God about what your ultimate goal should be, and what practical steps you will need to take to get there. You will include your Wise Advisors in this process. So again, if this were your situation, what would your goal be? What might your specific action steps look like?

For me, my goal would be to feel deep confidence in my great worth before God. I would simplify this into a short phrase: "Own my worth." I will take time every day to pray about owning my worth as God's child. Now, you might be wondering why I didn't make my goal, "Don't buy what you don't need." I would say because in this situation, that's not the real issue. It's a secondary cause of a much bigger picture. I will include it in my action list, yes. I will pray to be aware of all of my triggers surrounding my overspending. But my ultimate goal is to feel secure and valued *from within*. That is my true goal, what I most need to feel in order to find real healing.

After I landed on my true goal, I would intentionally go after my challenge with God. My personal list might look something like this:
1. Write my spiritual truths down and read them daily.
2. Memorize one or two scriptures to encourage me when I'm struggling.
3. Cancel my credit cards and cut them up immediately.
4. Call (insert name of Wise Advisor) whenever I'm feeling tempted.
5. Avoid situations and/or people who lure me from honoring God with my decisions.
6. Pray for the strength to remove myself from the situation when I'm tempted to overspend.
7. Find emotionally healthy activities that help me feel good about me.

And if my spending was a true addiction, I would add:
8. Join a spiritually based support group.
9. Seek professional counseling to help me find my core challenges more quickly.

Notice my list included short-term solutions, such as cutting up my credit cards, and having a specific, immediate plan in place for the moments when I struggle. There are also long-term solutions, such as internalizing God's view of me, and surrounding myself with people who will support me on my journey. Finding different activities that build into my spirit is definitely aligned with my God-given goal of owning my worth, whether it's volunteering at a homeless shelter once a week, joining a book club, or taking up yoga. My list will be adjusted as I go, adding some items and taking some off as need be. But ultimately, my goal is to learn to find my joy in God because unlike that five-dollar bargain, His love for me will last forever.

This exercise might have felt easy, or it might have felt like easier said than done, particularly if this happened to be your own personal tunnel. The truth is our own tunnel always feels challenging. If it weren't, we wouldn't be there in the first place! Someone else may say, "Well, just quit doing this," or, "You just need understand that." Remember, you can't change you, but God can. King David tells us in Psalm 37:4-6, "Take delight in the Lord, and he will give you the desires of your heart. Commit your way to the Lord, trust in him and he will do this: He will make your righteous reward shine like the dawn, your vindication like the noonday sun."

DEEPEN YOUR TRUST

In fact, trust in God is a huge part of being intentional. Trust tells me God has my back, that He has my best interests at heart. It reminds me that He wants good things for me. As I started intentionally working through my own tunnel, I had to also learn to trust where God was leading me. What I had in mind as I started was quite different from where God would ultimately lead me.

If I circle back to my situation of underemployment as an illustration, the upfront, obvious solution for me was to go back to being an elementary school teacher. Initially, in fact, that was my plan. Yet one of my part-time jobs as I finished my Master's degree was selling insurance. I began to experience strong success in the field.

At first, I thought maybe God was just blessing me financially because He knew my heart and what I was trying to accomplish. After all, I was crying out to and wrestling with Him about it every day. But after a while, I began to realize I had a God-given knack for sales. Who knew? Obviously, God did; it just took me some time to come on board with Him. So, after a lot of prayerful consideration, and consulting with my Wise Advisors, I opted to sell insurance full-time after graduation. I began to realize it would be the more flexible choice in terms of my time and would yield more income over the long haul—two of my big priorities.

In that situation, I learned the importance of allowing God to lead me to different places than I would have thought to go originally. If anyone had told me a few years earlier I would be starting an insurance business and making that my career, I would have scoffed at such an idea. Even deciding to work a straight commission job with no guaranteed income in my situation seemed crazy to many around me. Yet from the moment I made the decision to trust God's leading and sell insurance full-time, my financial picture began to positively change. It was abundantly clear I was on the right path.

There is a great scripture about this in Proverbs 16:9. It says, "A man's heart plans his way, but the Lord directs his steps." If God makes clear to you He wants you to zig when all along you thought you should zag, trust Him. Your intentional choices get you moving forward, yes, but allow God to show up and direct you toward His plan as you go. He will bless this kind of faith.

Sometimes the decisions we are called to make can be extremely difficult. As I was wading through how I would meet my financial obligations in the interim, I prayed about and tried many things. For me, the intentional decision I felt that God was directing me to was simply not something I was willing to do.

For months, many people I trusted and respected had been telling me to declare bankruptcy. I have deep convictions about the importance of being financially responsible and paying my debts. I had even taught classes on budgeting and finance prior to my ordeal. In other words, I had a lot of pride wrapped around this issue.

Finally, after much urging, I consulted a bankruptcy attorney. I had prayerfully and intentionally tackled this issue prior to going. I learned through research that if I could get out of debt in five years, paying off that debt was the best financial path to take. If it took longer than that, I would declare bankruptcy. I walked into the law office that day with my very detailed, well laid out plan of how I should *just* be able to get out of debt in five years if I was extremely diligent. I was determined to make that my path. The only reason I went there in the first place was to run my list by the man and make sure I was on track. That, and to get my Wise Advisors off my back.

I remember how patiently the attorney listened to my story about how I had gotten to where I was and my plan to get myself out of debt. He smiled at me with the heart of a father and asked, "You're German, aren't you?"

Not entirely sure where he was going with this, I sheepishly answered, "On my mother's side, yes."

He smiled. He said, "I know you. You have a strong work ethic. You give your best in all you do. You're that woman who puts everybody else's needs before your own. You're stubborn; you're determined, and those are good qualities." He leaned forward and continued, "But everything you've just shared with me in your plan requires consistent child support. Yet you just finished telling me that wasn't happening."

I quickly rushed in to explain why I thought this time would be different, why I thought I should start receiving consistent support. I will never forget the look on his face. It was full of deep compassion. He continued, "You mentioned you have three children. How old are they?" So, I told him.

Then he said, "On an airplane, the flight attendant announces that in case of an emergency and the cabin loses pressure, an oxygen mask will come down above you. Do you know what they say next?" Tears filled my eyes and I could no longer form words, because I knew where he was going with this. He continued, "Put your own oxygen mask on first before you help your child. They say this because if you pass out, there's no way you can help your children with theirs." I broke down and sobbed. I knew he was right. I couldn't help my children without taking care of myself first. I needed to put on my own financial oxygen mask if I was going to effectively be able to take care of my kids.

Now, I *am* a stubborn German, so it took a few more months of fighting and wrestling to surrender to the direction I already knew I was meant to take. I waited to see if I might be right about consistent child support coming in. I wasn't. It didn't. I had to swallow my pride and take that leap.

Ironically, making that intentional decision would become one of the most liberating choices I would make, and not in the way you would expect. Yes, I was finally able to meet my financial obligations now that I no longer had credit card debt that was the size of a mortgage payment. I no longer had to charge food, necessities and gas. But when I became someone who had declared bankruptcy, there was an odd sense of freedom in it. The sun still rose and set. My friends and family still loved me; and most importantly, God consistently reminded me I was still valued and honored in His sight. Plus, the lessons I learned internally through the process were priceless. It lent meaning and dignity to my struggle.

I'm not sure what your life lessons have been or are going to be. And I'm certainly not saying my solutions should be your solutions. In fact, you may feel led to do the exact opposite. What I am saying is that being intentional can be hard. The best solution is oftentimes not the easiest one. As we lean into God for His direction, He will ask us to take risks. Some of us never move forward, never take a step because we're so afraid of failing. What I learned was even though I may have failed in one particular battle, God was still going to win the overall war for me. In other words, my life was still going to be blessed, and it has been. Through time and patience, I have created savings, bought a home and have begun saving again for retirement. I'm able to help my children to do the same. I have come to understand my mistakes are my best teachers, so with God by my side I am able to push past my fear. His solutions work, so I trust Him.

TACKLING NEEDINESS

These are lessons I've sometimes learned the hard way. That's because when it comes to intentionality, you can't overlook the role neediness plays in your decision-making. When you're hurting, you feel needy. That's just how it is. But be aware this makes you very vulnerable to bad decisions in a desperate need to feel better, to feel like you belong. This can show up in overeating, withdrawing, reaching for that bottle, jumping into the next relationship without ever having healed or worked through the challenges of the last one, being safe instead of taking risks so you can grow, and the list goes on.

Remember, being intentional means bravely addressing both the internal and external challenges of our tunnels. Admitting we're needy requires us to quit trying to convince ourselves we're further along than we really are, or that people don't really understand. Trust me when I say I'm a deeply wired, very thoughtful person. Nearly all my mistakes with neediness came from a genuine belief I wasn't as needy and as vulnerable as I really was. Be aware of this.

I tend to be a generally positive person, and I tend to prefer action. Great qualities, both. But as I've learned, usually on the flipside of our strengths we find our weaknesses. Since I'm typically positive and prefer action, I have a tendency to think I'm doing better than I really am. I tend to move before I'm truly ready, or when *I* think I should instead of checking in with God and letting Him lead me. After knocking myself into some pretty hard walls a few times, I've finally learned to embrace my neediness, and embrace my need to trust God to direct my path. I made the intentional decision to quit going it on my own.

I can't share that without adding there are times when God asks me to move with intentionality, and I *don't* feel generally positive and ready. My heart can flood with fear because it feels like I'm being asked to jump off a cliff where all I can see below is a heavy mist. I have no idea where I'll be landing. Interestingly, it has been in those types of moments I have experienced the biggest blessings and growth in my life, so much so that I've really come to welcome them in a shaky, knee-wobbling way. I've learned the importance of taking that leap into the unknown.

Harking all the way back to the time I shared about buying a meal for a homeless couple when I was dead broke, leaps of faith take us to new places. They are almost always the first, important step in a much greater journey that we can't completely understand or even conceive of yet. By seeking connection with and vision from God, we are able to trust in God enough to take those brave and intentional first steps, even when they don't always make sense to us.

By now, you will have taken some time to figure out your tunnel, what your internal challenges are and what triggers them, and how to replace your lies with God's spiritual truths. Now it's time to ask yourself what's your big goal? What's your action plan? What are some smaller, manageable steps to achieving this goal? What will your very first (or next) step be? How might you need to modify your plan as you move forward? As you begin to intentionally construct your goals and plans with God, use the summary below as a guidepost. Remember that just like everything we've talked about so far, you will face obstacles. Growth is rarely straight forward, and that's okay.

I want to leave you with a final scripture to consider as you begin taking your first intentional steps. In Ephesians 6:16-18 it says:

> Be prepared. You're up against far more than you can handle on your own. Take all the help you can get, every weapon God has issued, so that when it's all over but the shouting you'll still be on your feet. Truth, righteousness, peace, faith, and salvation are more than words. Learn how to apply them. You'll need them throughout your life. God's Word is an indispensable weapon. In the same way, prayer is essential in this ongoing warfare. Pray hard and long. Pray for your brothers and sisters. Keep your eyes open. Keep each other's spirits up so that no one falls behind or drops out.

What I love about this scripture, besides the way it reminds me of how powerful the weapons God gives me are, is that it lets me know that I'll still be standing on my feet at the end of my challenge. Put differently, I won't just survive the ordeal I'm going through; I will stand tall when it's done, better for the process. By creating a vision, connecting with God and with others, and bravely and intentionally tackling your internal and external challenges, you will experience such victory, too.

SUMMARY

As you tackle your own tunnel, listen to God's direction. Approach your challenges one by one, both internally and externally. Invite God into the process. Decide on your big goal or goals. Make sure any goal you make respects your overall God-given priorities (family, sense of self, etc.). Then simplify your goal and pray for it daily.

Choose the intentional order of your steps after praying and seeking advice, focusing on what most needs to happen first. Be sure to include your Wise Advisor(s) in your process. Then, break down each goal into small, manageable steps that you can work on one at a time. Be sure you're experiencing some success in one area before you move on to the next.

Be aware that God's design may not always be the easiest or the most logical, but it *is* the one that works. Trust His guidance. Proverb 11:23 tells us, "The desire of the righteous ends only in good." In time, you *will* see the fruit of your efforts.

FOR FURTHER THOUGHT

1. Set aside time this week to prayerfully decide what your first big goal should be.
2. How does your big goal fit into your God-given priorities?
3. What do you see as being the biggest obstacle(s) to your goal? Why is that?
4. Who is someone you can go to for help with your challenge? How will you approach them?
5. What is one scripture you can memorize to help you when you need it?

CHALLENGE

In those moments where my bravery and intentionality are being put to the test, whether by neediness or fear, one of my favorite scriptures is found in Isaiah 44:2-5:

Don't be afraid, I've redeemed you. I've called your name. You're mine. When you're in over your head, I'll be there with you. When you're in rough waters, you will not go down. When you're between a rock and a hard place, it won't be a dead end—Because I am God, your personal God, the Holy of Israel, your Savior. I paid a huge price for you: all of Egypt, with rich Cush and Seba thrown in! That's how much I love you! I'd sell off the whole world to get you back, trade the creation just for you. So don't be afraid: I'm with you.

Read that scripture again, but this time insert your name in there every sentence or two. It's powerful, isn't it? Whenever you're feeling weak, do this exercise.

CHAPTER 7

FIGHTING THE CAVE-INS
Consistency

"It's not what we do once in a while that shapes our lives.
It's what we do consistently." — Anthony Robbins

I once had this very vivid dream. I was in a mini-van full of people. I have no idea where we were heading nor do I remember who was in the van with me, but I do remember this: I was supposed to drive. So in my dream, I sat down in the driver's seat, put the key in the ignition, started the car, and began to drive. I was not going particularly fast. Then for some inexplicable reason, I got up and moved to the very back of the van. I guess I was just tired of driving. The van was still moving but no one was at the wheel. I started yelling at someone who was closer to the steering wheel to jump into the driver's seat and drive. The van was moving erratically, but everyone was looking at me with horror, expecting me to get back in the driver's seat. Even though I was farthest away from the steering wheel, I was the only one who moved to take back control of the van.

At first in my dream, I was upset at the others in the van for not moving to the driver's seat. After all, they were closer. It was easier for them to quickly take the wheel, and it gave us the quickest route to save ourselves. Then it dawned on me—why did I get out of the driver's seat to begin with? I was the one who was *supposed* to be driving. Why would I just get up and go to the back of the van like that? Where was my head? I woke up in fear.

As I sat there pondering this dream, pieces of it began to become clear and I realized a few very important things: My life was the van, and no one else was going to drive it for me. I could pull over and rest, certainly. I could use maps and other tools to help me go in the right direction. But I couldn't abdicate my life to someone else so they could live it for me without disastrous consequences.

I think we all have moments where we wish someone else would just do the driving or the heavy lifting in our lives. We want the fun, happy parts; we don't want to have to deal with the hard, ugly ones. Consistency is all about helping us to develop the habits we need to make it through the hard parts of the journey, and ultimately to enjoy the beautiful parts that much more because of it.

I have to start any kind of discussion on consistency by immediately disclosing that I think I'm horrible at it. To begin with, for years I thought of consistency as some kind of straightjacket, a habit that would make life boring, predictable and dull. I didn't want to do the same thing day in and day out for the rest of my life. Nothing wrong with it per se; it just wasn't me.

It took me time to realize consistency can have many different definitions, and that even my desire to constantly try new things was a *consistent* quality in my life. It was a way of acting or reacting that I consistently went to. It's like Goths (or Punkers back in my day). They want to be different, to stand out from the crowd. Yet they are in absolute conformity in how they look as a group. They are the same in their differentness. This idea of my decisions driving me began to challenge how I viewed the idea of consistency.

I decided to check out what God had to say about consistency. Guess what? Couldn't find it. Not a single instance. Couldn't find a reference to the word "consistent" either. Now I'm sure there's some version out there that may use those words, but in going through my NIV Bible, I couldn't find a single one. With further exploring, I realized the Bible uses different words for this idea of consistency than we do—discipline, wisdom, hard work, and righteousness just to name a few. It also uses antonyms—sluggard, laziness, wanton, etc. More intriguingly, I began to find this idea of a path.

Consider the following from Proverbs:
… in all your ways acknowledge Him and He will make your paths straight. (3:6)
I guide you in the way of wisdom and lead you along straight paths. (4:11)
Make level paths for your feet and take only ways that are firm. (4:26)
For a man's ways are in full view of the Lord, and He examines all his paths. (5:21)
Leave your simple ways and you will live. Walk in the way of understanding. (9:6)
In the way of righteousness there is life; along that path is immortality. (12:28)
The way of the sluggard is blocked with thorns, but the path of the upright is a highway. (15:19)

The word "path" or "paths" is actually mentioned in the Bible over one hundred times.

I've finally come to realize that God is deeply interested in helping us along on our path, our life journey; and while we may be tempted to want to get out of the driver's seat when our journey gets tough, if we consistently lean into God, our path will stay clear longer, we'll get past obstacles more quickly, and we'll stumble and fall less often. It doesn't mean we get a pass on life's challenges. Rather, He promises to guide us on to something even greater in the midst of them

With that in mind, consistency is really more about learning how to always examine the path we're on and how we're walking on our journey, listening to God for direction on how to move forward, and trusting that He'll correct us if we're veering off in a wrong direction, because we're in relationship with Him. For our purposes, let's define consistency as training for the important step of developing and maintaining healthy habits by consistently walking with God.

For many of us, the world has taught us to not believe we can develop and maintain healthy habits. After all, we've tried the latest diet book, but the weight came back—or never left in the first place. We vowed we would quit dating people who are bad for us, yet we find ourselves in yet another messy relationship. I believe that's because the way the world tells us to change is fractured and ineffective. That's why there's not just one diet book or one self-help book that everyone in the world clings to. They don't really work! They begin with the faulty premise that it's up to you to change yourself through your own self-discipline. In fact, some researchers put the failure rate of such an approach at 97%.[1] Yet we keep trying it over and over again, doing the same things but expecting a different result—which some define as insanity.

Consistently working through our challenges with God is much different. It sets us up for real growth. There is a scripture I love in 1 John 2:15-17 that says, "Don't love the world's ways. Don't love the world's goods. Love of the world squeezes out love for the Father. Practically everything that goes on in the world—wanting your own way, wanting everything for yourself, wanting to appear important—has nothing to do with the Father. It just isolates you from him. The world and all its wanting, wanting, wanting is on the way out—but whoever does what God wants is set for eternity." I like the idea of being set for eternity. It starts with doing it God's way.

Unlike the world, God's way isn't always very linear. We think that if we do steps A, B, and C, life will improve and we'll naturally reach our goal. I have yet to find that to be true. I seem to start in with God on step A, only to have Him jump me up to step C, back to A, then start on B, notice there's a step B2 I hadn't even considered, and so on. In other words, it tends to be messy; I tend to take as many steps backward and sideways as I do forward, but somehow, over time, I find myself transformed, different. I realize God taught me some incredible lessons in all of that zigging and zagging. Then

I step back and marvel at how God's plan works every time, even when it doesn't always make sense to me in the moment.

The greatest driver behind meaningful change in my life has truly been God's love. Back in my late teens and early twenties, when I was first learning what it meant to walk with God, it was His love for me that overwhelmed me and motivated me to change. When I understood in a deep way what God had truly done for me on the cross with His son, and how much He had to love me to be willing to allow that kind of sacrifice, even in the midst of my mess, I was blown away. It still makes me tear up to think of it.

God's love for you is deep and profound. The more you tie into God's love for you, and into His incredible mercy and grace, the more you will find yourself growing and changing in ways you can't even imagine yet, despite yourself. Paul described it this way: "For Christ's love compels us, because we are convinced that one died for all, and therefore all died. And Christ did die for all of us. He died so we would no longer live for ourselves, but for the one who died and was raised to life for us" (2 Corinthians 5:14-15). It is God's love that compels us to be different; not our own self will (or lack thereof).

Sometimes falling flat on our faces, regardless of the whys, can be a remarkable gift. For me, when nearly everything I valued and defined myself by was stripped away, I saw God, standing in the midst of my rubble. He wasn't embarrassed by me; He wasn't ashamed of me, even though in my mind He should have been. Instead, there He was—offering His unconditional love and acceptance, stretching out His hand to help lift me up, and hold me in His arms emotionally. He helped me brush off the dust, and chart a new and better course for my life. In that moment of worthlessness, He told me I was worthy. In my moments of crippling despair, He reminded me of His unfailing love and gave me back my hope. Like King David before me, I realized, "you make your saving help my shield, and your right hand sustains me; you stoop down to make me great" (Psalm 18:35).

Love for God is what will develop consistency within you. Again, it may not always be straightforward in our minds, but God's ways are perfect and they work. Remember how we talked about how important it was to connect with God? Consistency emerges from taking those next steps in your relationship with God and learning to lean into Him even more, and continuing to do so long after we've emerged from our tunnel. If we're going to allow God to really change us, it first and foremost starts with developing the healthy habit of walking consistently with Him.

Now if you were raised in a legalistic, religious environment, "consistently walking with God" could have been turned into some kind of rigid ritual that requires you to spend x amount of time in prayer and the reading of scripture each day, or else you're being disobedient. Or it may conjure up visions of monasteries or some sort of super spirituality. That's not what we're talking about here. Your relationship with God should be just that—a relationship. I have days when I don't get a chance to talk deeply with the people I love, and days where we get to spend huge chunks of time together. But here is where the consistency comes in—they're not far away from my heart and my mind. It's rare for me to *not* think about them each day. They matter to me in a real way, and it shows in my *actions* and my *time*.

Jesus is a great example of this. One of the first things he taught publically was how to pray. His follower Luke tells us in Luke 5:16, "But Jesus often withdrew to lonely places and prayed." Paul tells us in Hebrews 5:7, "During the days of Jesus' life on earth, he offered up prayers and petitions with fervent cries and tears to the one who could save him from death, and he was heard because of his reverent submission." Jesus also quoted scripture often. It was his habit to answer questions and challenges by expanding on scriptures. How was he able to do this? It implies he read his Bible (or to be more accurate, the Torah) a lot.

We explored how to develop a relationship with God in Chapter 2 on Connection (go back and re-read that section if necessary). Consistency enters in as we begin to build the healthy habit of connecting with God on a regular basis through reading and prayer. We don't just reach out to God when we want something or we're a mess, though many of us certainly start there (which is okay). Instead, connecting to God needs to become an important piece of how we process and navigate along our path, a steady rhythm we put in place.

For most of us, either Bible reading or prayer will come more naturally than the other. We'll have the tendency to lean more heavily on the one that's easiest. Still, we need both. Think of reading as God talking to you, and praying as you talking to God. You need both to have a healthy relationship.

Like any healthy life rhythm, the more we can make our time with God a part of our daily routine, the easier it becomes to make time to connect with Him. The more you know Him, the more you want to be with Him. Some people pray in the shower and listen to the Bible on MP3 on their way to work. Some have a specific spot they sit in every morning or evening to pray and read. It doesn't really matter where or how; it just matters that you do.

When it comes to reading, you can read a Psalm or a chapter of a New Testament book each day. Keep a journal to write about what you're learning or even write out your prayers. This is particularly helpful because you can look back over time and see ways God guided you or answered a specific prayer. You can also buy short devotional guides online or in stores to help you explore the Bible and understand it more. There is a wealth of free resources online as well. Pick one and start (revisit the end of Chapter Three on Connection for more ideas).

Personally, I've found that a great way to connect with God is to simply talk with Him as if I'm talking with my best friend or the perfect dad. Share with him what you're feeling, what you're concerned about, and what you and others need help with. Keep your heart and your mind in the process, fighting off distractions. Then always take time to listen to His response.

Remember our discussion about learning to listen to those little nudges God gives us? As we begin to listen, God is able to show up more and more and speak to us. Pastor Rick Warren has a great way of describing this process:

> The Bible says, "Be still and know that I am God" (Psalm 46:10). That means sit down and shut up. That's how you hear God and get near to God. You have to sit alone and just be quiet with your Bible and say, "God, is there anything you want to say to me?" You read God's Word, and you talk to him about what's on your heart.

To me, that's the best way to approach God—naturally, in a manner that allows Him to be seen by you genuinely and authentically. If a prayer acronym helps you find that connection, use it. Many people find them to be a valuable tool. You can find several great prayer acronyms online if you'd like to try a new one or you're not sure what one is. If an acronym doesn't help, don't use it. Again, the key is simply to make that time to connect *consistently*.

As you grow in your walk with God, you will find many varied ways to connect with Him, just like any strong relationship you have. Some people call the way they connect with God "spiritual disciplines." I think of them more simply, as just creative ways to draw close to my maker, and I lump them into two categories: *In* and *Up*.

In is all about doing things that allow me to look inwardly to who God is calling me to be. I may choose to fast, or go without something (food, music, chocolate, sugar, etc.), so that in the moments I miss whatever it is I'm fasting from, it reminds me to think of God and His presence in my life. I take that time or moment to pray. Sometimes it's having deep talks with my Wise Advisor(s) about what I see in my character, asking for their input and guidance.

It could be spending time in silence, or retreating away somewhere to connect with God and reflect. Perhaps it's doing a random act of kindness, and not letting anyone else know. *In* is all about surrendering to God's will over mine, and seeking His direction.

Out is engaging with God in ways that are meaningful. It can time spent in prayer, to praise and thank Him for all He has done. It could be singing songs to him, or dancing before Him. It could be as simple as lying on your back under the stars, and allowing yourself to marvel at the work of His hands. *Out* takes a moment to stop and acknowledge the beauty and strength of God, and to worship and honor Him.

Another great *Out* activity is to find ways to serve others. When you're in a tunnel, it's easy to get tunnel vision; all you see is your own challenges. Getting out and helping others, whether at a homeless shelter, a food pantry, or taking your elderly neighbor to dinner, reminds you of your blessings; it allows you to connect with others and let go of your situation for a time. You will need to be more inwardly focused during times of trial, by necessity, but don't underestimate the importance of still making time to give back in the ways you can.

By growing in our walk with God, we begin to create a rhythm in our lives of consistent growth in every area. By focusing both *In* and *Out*, because we need both, we learn to hear and see our maker in richer ways. These concepts are the foundational structure for true, transformative change in our lives. They are the backbone of the healthy habits we are allowing God to create within us.

As we grow in developing consistent, good habits in our walk with God, the next step is to evaluate how we're doing along our path. We've spent a lot of time now talking about what that might look like. As you look back on the principles we've discussed—Vision, Connection, Bravery, finding Wise Advisors, Intentionality and creating specific, concrete, measurable steps—what are you learning about you so far? Take a moment to write it down.

Pause and reflect on your list. Is there anything you need to go back and dig into again? Is it time to refine your vision? Have you taken any concrete steps yet? How have those steps gone? Have you created any way to measure your progress? Have you been intentional about including God in the process? Write down your answers here as well.

If you've been intentional, in some areas you will see progress. You will see ways you are growing and evolving to become who God has called you to be. In other areas, you likely won't. Maybe you haven't taken that first step yet, or when you did, it didn't go the way you anticipated. Or it could be your vision isn't as clear as it first was, or you have yet to find intentional solutions. That's okay. Remember: True, God-directed change isn't a straight line. You won't always go smoothly from point A to point B. Success rarely looks like this:

It usually looks something more like this:

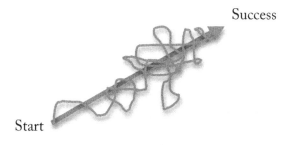

Be patient with yourself. Extend yourself grace, just as God does. Remember His word of encouragement to you: "My grace is enough to cover and sustain you. My power is made perfect in weakness," (2 Corinthians 12:9). Keep allowing God to forge on ahead of you. Pull in your Wise Advisors. Continue leaning into God. He will deliver you.

Remember—consistency involves developing something, and developing involves training. None of us pick up a baseball bat and immediately understand how to play every aspect of the game. It takes patient practice over time, taking on new skills as we master older ones. Spiritual growth and consistency work the same way. I Corinthians 9:25 tells us, "Athletes in training are very strict with themselves, exercising self-control over desires, and for what? For a wreath that soon withers or is crushed or simply forgotten. That is not our race. We run for the crown that we will wear for eternity." Be brave and keep reaching for that bat. God Himself will teach you over time how to swing more and more effectively.

CONSISTENCY CHALLENGES

For some of you, when I asked you to write out your answers to certain questions, you may have looked down at a mostly blank page if you wrote anything at all. I get it. You're beginning to understand the challenges that come with consistency and the whole boldly shining process—you have to create space to put into place what you're learning. And if you don't take time to evaluate with God how it's going (a great way to do so is in your time with Him, by the way), you won't move forward on your path out of your tunnel. We face two obstacles here: time and effort. Let's start with time.

TIME

Time is a finite thing. Once it's gone, it's gone. God tells us, "You are a mist that appears for a little while and then vanishes" (James 4:14). During times of struggle you may wish you could vanish for a while. I understand. I was, after all, the one dreaming of having someone else take over the driving for me. I was tired. I was stressed. I had been pushed far beyond the edge of anything I thought I could endure. I was always working, or trying to be present for my kids. Time wasn't overly plentiful. When I did get it, I usually wanted to collapse in a heap on my bed—or the couch, or anywhere I happened to be sitting.

The one thing that kept drawing me back to making the time was, once again, God's love. I knew, better than anyone else in my life, that God understood my challenges. He accepted me along with my messy emotions, traitorous thoughts, and lack of energy. He reminded me, "There is no fear in love. But perfect love drives out fear" (John. 4:18). He wasn't mad if I had a bad day and needed to emotionally retreat for a while. He got it.

Yet within that I also knew I needed to make time with Him. If I had never forced myself off the couch to reach for something better, I would have continued to experience the same dead-end, life-sucking conclusions I found myself in. Believe you me, I felt desperate. I knew the only way I could successfully get through my tunnel was with God. It meant some late nights and early mornings sometimes. I learned to eat and pray very effectively. Time in the shower allowed me to cry to God without my children being any the wiser that I was breaking down. I also mastered the "I'm taking a short nap" routine with a locked bedroom door so I could silently cry and get my heart out with my Father in a way that didn't scare my kids. But because I was desperate, I made time.

What I have come to understand is that carving out space for growth, at its heart, really isn't about making time. For me, time is often the excuse I use because I don't want to get my brave on and be messy. I don't want to have to face me. Usually, we avoid making time for God because dealing with our issues is scary. We fear the cost. Re-read the chapter on bravery if you need to, but remember—being willing to face what is uncomfortable comes from knowing that what God has in store for you is worth that price. The more you begin to realize that facing your fears with God actually *frees* you of the very things that hold you down, it's hard to *not* make time for God consistently, all the time, wherever you are. He becomes invaluable in your life. Let His love and His power drive away your fear; don't let time become your excuse.

LACK OF ENERGY

When you intentionally land on that one big goal you made with God, and you know it's His goal for your life, it will guide you. It will push you forward when you'd rather sit back. The Holy Spirit will nudge you until you move. That isn't to say there won't be times you choose to ignore it. But what you'll find is the more you listen for God's guidance and follow it, the happier you will be. You'll find you're more centered, and you have more energy to keep moving through your tunnel.

Making effort is all about energy. When you're struggling, your strength is diminished. That's why we've emphasized nurturing yourself and doing things that fill you, and focused on being brave when you don't feel like driving your life and the car is going in all sorts of crazy directions. Be patient with yourself. But intentionally set up expectations, however small, and work toward them one step at a time. Sometimes we need to let God tell us some hard truths to develop consistency. Usually we need His encouragement. God gives us both through His word when we search for it.

I'll be honest with you. There are times I feel lazy. I'm overwhelmed, tired. I want to be rescued instead of having to make the effort of working through my challenges. I just want God to fix it, take it away, and pull me into a better place. I've never had God answer that prayer for me. He allows me to have my moments, of course. We all need to allow ourselves to feel what it is we're feeling; but God doesn't rescue us from our growth process. And when I've sought to arrange my own rescue, it's never gone well. It's always led me to an emotional dead end.

In those moments of personal laziness, one of my favorite truth scriptures is found in Proverbs 6:6-11. It says, "Take a lesson from the ant, you who love leisure and ease. Observe how it works, and dare to be just as wise. It has no boss, no one laying down the law or telling it what to do. Yet it gathers its food through summer and takes what it needs from the harvest. How long do you plan to lounge your life away, you lazy fool? Will you ever get out of bed? You say, 'A little sleep, a little rest, a few more minutes, a nice little nap.'

But soon poverty will be on top of you like a robber; need will assault you like a well-armed warrior."

Did I mention consistency is not my strength? This scripture helps me in those moments when I don't want to move. Perfect love may drive out fear, but the Bible teaches that fear is the beginning of knowledge. There are times I *need* to fear my lack of action because of the dire consequences it can cause. Those consequences can be very big—eviction notices, losing a job, losing your kids, etc. But they can also be insidiously small. When you allow yourself to stay trapped, you can look up and realize years of your life have slipped by you, never to return, and nothing about you or your situation is different. So, while it's not where I want to live, sometimes I need to visit fear to remember there are ramifications to my choices. This is the healthy kind of fear we talked about in the chapter on bravery.

Laziness may not be your issue, but one thing I do know—you have one. We all do. Even the Apostle Paul did, which he shares about in 2 Corinthians 12:7-10:

> *...so I wouldn't get a big head, I was given the gift of a handicap to keep me in constant touch with my limitations. Satan's angel did his best to get me down; what he in fact did was push me to my knees. No danger then of walking around high and mighty! At first I didn't think of it as a gift, and begged God to remove it. Three times I did that, and then he told me, "My grace is enough; it's all you need. "My strength comes into its own in your weakness."*
>
> *Once I heard that, I was glad to let it happen. I quit focusing on the handicap and began appreciating the gift. It was a case of Christ's strength moving in on my weakness. Now I take limitations in stride, and with good cheer, these limitations that cut me down to size—abuse, accidents, opposition, bad breaks. I just let Christ take over! And so the weaker I get, the stronger I become.*

It is our challenges and weaknesses that drive us to our knees and allow God to show up and help us grow in ways we aren't able to do on our own. Now when people tell me how impressed they are at all I get accomplished (which still amazes me), I know without a doubt that's God doing His thing in my life. In and of myself, that stuff just wouldn't have happened—not to that extent. Find those scriptures that really speak to your area(s) of weakness and let them be a healthy reminder when you need it.

Remember, ultimately it is God's grace, His love that is the greatest motivator. Where I most consistently want to live is under the shelter of God's wings, knowing His love protects me and keeps me strong. It is my positive truths that I most often surround myself with. Probably my favorite Psalm when I'm feeling beat up and in need of encouragement is Psalm 18. There are so many great verses, but I'll share with you a taste: "He reached down from on high and took hold of me; he drew me out of deep waters. He rescued me from my powerful enemy, from my foes, who were too strong for me. They confronted me in the day of my disaster, but the Lord was my support. He brought me out into a spacious place; he rescued me because he delighted in me" (16-19). Whether you need grace and encouragement, challenging truth, or both to make time and get energy, use God's word to help guide you forward on your path toward consistent growth.

NEXT STEPS

If you have been digging in with God, refining your vision and slowly making brave, intentional steps forward, I know you're already beginning to feel God's hand at work in your life. You are beginning to experience first-hand what King Solomon shares in Proverbs 2:7: "He has success in store for the upright. He is their shield, protecting them and guarding their pathway." The two words I really want you to home in on are "success" and "shield." Consistently walking with God brings about successful change. The chapter on boldly shining will celebrate success, but for now, embrace these early victories, however small, and remember—now that your life is turned "upright" toward God, your successes will continue as long as you allow God to protect you.

A big part of consistency is, in fact, letting God protect and guard you along your path. It is crucial to consistently set aside time to evaluate and process your situation, how it's evolving, and ways God may be nudging you, particularly if they're in a different direction than originally anticipated. Your Wise Advisors should be a part of that process as well. Remember, the goal is to let God direct your steps, not to just run ahead with what you think is best. The Bible describes this as "abiding."

ABIDING WITH GOD

To abide in something means to hang tough, live with, stand for, defer or consent to. Abiding in God means you continue to allow Him to dwell in your life, to defer to His judgment, and to continue on your life's journey faithfully submitted to Him. Jesus says, "Abide in Me, and I will abide in you. A branch cannot bear fruit if it is disconnected from the vine, and neither will you if you are not connected to Me" (John 15:4). Aha. That connection word again. Abiding, connecting, remaining, and dwelling—whatever the word, the point is clear. You are not meant to live this life alone, left to your own devices. You are meant to allow God to be the fuel in your engine.

As I mentioned previously, I can be a stubborn German woman. Letting God protect and guide me requires me to let go of something I really love: control. Abiding in God is, by definition, deferring to someone else's judgment. In this case, the judge happens to be an all-powerful, all-knowing, all-seeing and deeply loving Father who knows and understands what I need far more than I do. Still, the human in me likes to think she knows best, and I have a hard time consistently surrendering. If you're at all like me—and I don't think I'm alone with this—understand that consistently abiding with God is going to require some wrestling on your part.

There is actually a rather interesting story in the Old Testament about a wrestling match I find helpful in growing consistency. I don't think anyone was wearing a really cool WWF costume or anything, but if pay per view were around, I think it would've been a huge hit. It all starts with this guy named Jacob. Now, Jacob was a trickster. He had already stolen his older twin brother Esau's birthright, which was a big deal back then because the oldest son inherited everything. Later, he also stole his father's blessing away from Esau. Esau planned to kill Jacob, so Jacob fled.

Interestingly, Jacob was declared at birth to be the one who would be in charge and receive God's blessing, even though it was against the culture of his day. But Jacob never trusted that. He manipulated; he cajoled. He didn't trust that he would receive blessing. Understand that God spoke to Jacob. He rescued Jacob more than once from precarious situations. Still, Jacob had a hard time trusting God.

More than twenty years later, Jacob was met by angels, and decided to send word to meet with Esau in order to reconcile with his brother. Esau accepted, but when Jacob learned he was bringing four hundred men with him, he panicked. He came up with an elaborate plan to keep everything he had safe. The Bible says he was "in great fear and distress" (Genesis 32:7). And no wonder. Esau had plenty of reasons to go after his younger brother.

In this moment of fear and doubt, Jacob did something I love. He dropped to his knees and prayed. He reminded God of His promise to bless Jacob, and humbly asked God to protect him. Still, in his heart Jacob was unsure.

Jacob was all alone on the eve before he was to meet his brother, when a man showed up. The man was no ordinary man, either, but an angel. Somehow, the two started wrestling. Jacob was no longer a young buck, but he refused to quit. These two literally wrestled until dawn. The angel finally tapped into his supernatural power to dislocate Jacob's hip, and still Jacob would not let go! Why? He wanted a blessing. He wanted to know he would be all right (a blessing he received, by the way—Esau greeted him with joyful tears).

I can relate to Jacob. God has shown me time and again that He has my back, that He loves me and will protect me. Yet there I am, down on the floor wrestling with my emotions and fears late into the night. I can argue with God and fight with Him. I remind Him of things that He clearly doesn't need to be reminded of, though, of course, I do. I have a hard time trusting He will do all He has promised, even though He has always been faithful to me. I have found this to be especially true when He changes my preconceived notion of where I think my path should go.

It's in those moments of doubt and testing that I have learned the importance of continuing to wrestle, to never surrender. I've definitely lost some matches here and there. I've taken my lumps. But I've also learned the power of consistently getting back in the ring, of refusing to let my own inner battles keep me from seeing God's hand. It can be a real battle to let Him in. Yet the more I learn to keep wrestling until I receive and believe God's blessing, the less I have to wrestle. Faith built over time has taught me that God really is true to His word, whether or not I believe that in the moment.

While clearly God would have blessed Jacob without him having to wrestle through the night, God knew Jacob needed to wrestle. He knew Jacob would grow through the process. So, as you're working on consistency, don't quit wrestling. It's hard; it can be mentally exhausting. Take breaks when you need to, but don't you quit! When the dawn breaks—and it will break—you'll find yourself at a place of surrendered peace, trusting in God's blessing, and moving away from your tunnel.

The Apostle Peter tells us, "You have faith in God, whose power will protect you until the last day. Then he will save you, just as he has always planned to do. On that day you will be glad, even if you have to go through many hard trials for a while. Your faith will be like gold that has been tested in a fire. And these trials will prove that your faith is worth much more than gold that can be destroyed. When Jesus wraps this all up, it's your faith, not your gold, that God will have on display as evidence of his victory" (1 Peter 1:5-7). Consistently abiding with God may sometimes require some late-night wrestling matches, but the outcome in the form of His blessing is worth it.

Consistency will develop as you continue to wrestle with God, allowing Him to take over control of your life, and your situation as you abide in Him. I still have times where I feel like I keep reaching for God and nothing changes. In those moments, God has taught me to pray longer, to pray harder, to sometimes step back and rest, but to never quit. It's a process that is rarely immediate, but its results are shown in great growth over time. Replace the bad thoughts with positive ones consistently, and you're on the path toward boldly shining.

Hebrews 5:14 tells us, "Therefore, my dear brothers and sisters, stand firm. Let nothing move you. Always give yourselves fully to the work of the Lord, because you know that your labor in the Lord is not in vain." Even if your efforts to abide feel futile, they never are. Each attempt, whether you feel like it's moving you forward, backward or somewhere else entirely, ultimately drives you closer to God.

SUMMARY

Consistency comes from spending time with God, and developing healthy life rhythms with Him, looking both *In* and *Up*. Evaluate your steps with Him, and put into place what you're learning. Remember to extend yourself grace, seasoned with truth. Keep abiding with God, wrestling with Him through your struggles, so He can move you forward on your path.

FOR FURTHER THOUGHT

1.   Decide what you will do to continue to develop your walk with God. What routines will you put into place? What might be an obstacle to overcome? How will you overcome it?

2.   During your time with God this week, evaluate your steps. How did you feel during this process? Does anything need to be tweaked or refined? What are you learning about yourself?

3.   What will be your biggest obstacle to developing consistency in your life? How might you tackle it? What scriptures of grace and truth might be helpful for you?

4.   The great poet and writer Maya Angelou said, "One isn't necessarily born with courage, but one is born with potential. Without courage, we cannot practice any other virtue with consistency. We can't be kind, true, merciful, generous, or honest." What is one way you will need to be brave in order to be consistent?

REFERENCES

[1]Loyd, A. (2015). *Beyond Willpower*. New York, NY: Crown Publishing Group.

CHAPTER 8

KEEP DIGGING
Intentionality Toward Others

"Darkness cannot drive out darkness; only light can do that. Hate cannot drive out hate; only love can do that." — Martin Luther King, Jr.

Relationships are a key, salient ingredient in life. Creating them, maintaining them, defining them, and sometimes letting go of them take up an incredible amount of our time and energy throughout life. Yet they can be the most valuable, precious pieces of this existence we get to experience. No talk on intentionality would be complete without an honest discussion of what it means to be intentional with others.

Very few of us find ourselves in our tunnels all alone. Often, we carry family members, close friends and intimate relationships in there with us. Sometimes they follow us in when they shouldn't in a desire to help; sometimes we drag them in against their will. There are times when you and the ones you love have all been thrust into a situation that immediately creates a challenge all of you will need to work through, even though each one will still need to navigate through that tunnel in his or her own way.

I could write an entire book on being intentional with others, so great is its importance in our lives. My goal here is to get the conversation started, to begin to help you to bravely, consistently and intentionally approach the key relationships around you, even if they seem fractured beyond repair, so you can take those important steps toward healing.

When we begin to get intentional in our lives, it will impact how we view and treat others, including our friendships, our intimate relationships, and, for those of us with kids, our relationships with our children. Let's tackle these one at a time, always keeping in view the words Jesus shared when His followers felt like eternal change was impossible: "Jesus looked at them intently, then said, 'Without God, it is utterly impossible. But with God everything is possible'" (Mark 10:27).

BECOMING INTENTIONAL WITH OTHERS

We have already discussed what it means to set boundaries and exit relationships that have been toxic. Here we are examining very specifically how to potentially change relationships in which we view ourselves as the offending party.

The word the Bible uses to describe changing negative patterns is called repentance. Repentance is a religious word that simply means "to turn." You were headed down the wrong path, so you turn and go in a different direction. It could be a subtle change, or a complete turn-around. We've already covered what it means to turn and go in a different direction to get out of the tunnels we find ourselves in, and how to take responsibility for ourselves and our choices, since that's all we have control over.

Intentionality toward others is the next important step. Repentance with others involves turning away from detrimental behaviors (sins), and acknowledging and owning the negative impact we've left behind in our wake. Some examples of this might be that you've committed adultery, but you still want to try and save your marriage. Or you've been physically or verbally abusive to those you love, or lashed out in anger at your children. It could be you've been self-absorbed, for reasons good or bad, but either way your family feels neglected and unloved. Maybe as you've dug into the how and why behind your tunnel, you've come to realize you're not a very good friend to people, or you're always judging them through the lens of your own insecurity. Whatever the situation, there's been collateral damage to those around you. Let's explore what it looks like to repent, to turn away from negative behavior patterns with the people we care about and love, by taking a closer look at how the Bible describes this idea of repentance.

Repentance can be a misunderstood concept, especially by the religious. I've heard it described as taking a U-turn, or moving away in the opposite direction (which it can sometimes mean). I've seen repentance combined with the idea of penance, which means to punish yourself emotionally and sometimes even physically for "sins" or bad deeds you've committed. In other words, do "x" amount of (fill in the blank) and you can earn your forgiveness or prove your true sorrow. I've also seen repentance become a way of burdening people with unrealistic expectations and demands that become crushing, often turning those very same people away from the love and vision Christ has for them in the first place. There are many warped ways of thinking about repentance that permeate some church cultures.

We are told in Isaiah 30:15, "This is what the Sovereign Lord, the Holy One of Israel, says: 'In repentance and rest is your salvation, in quietness and trust is your strength.'" God is letting us know that when we turn toward a better way and rest in His amazing grace, quietly trusting God to heal and change us—versus throwing out a lot of words trying to announce to people that we are different—we find strength. Part of how God saves us from our dark tunnels is by helping us to turn away from our idea of what we should do, and quietly allow God to take over and direct us through His word, His Spirit, and the people He's put in our lives to help guide us.

God speaks to us again in Jeremiah 8:6 about this idea of going our own way, doing what we think is best, instead of really tuning into His will: "I listen carefully, but none of you admit that you've done wrong. Without a second thought, you run down the wrong road like cavalry troops charging into battle." When you've hurt people, one of the best first steps you can take toward change is to slow down enough to truly figure out what you've done wrong to others, and own it. Again, this is why it's so important to understand and work through the drivers behind your actions, as we discussed in Bravery and Intentionality. You can't own what you don't see or acknowledge. You can't turn your horse around, so to speak, if you don't realize what direction you need to start going in.

If, for example, you've committed adultery, you need to understand *why*, looking beyond the obvious of finding someone else physically appealing or emotionally supportive. If you've been abusive, angry and impatient, a poor friend, a negligent parent, or a selfish lover, whatever it is you've been learning about yourself throughout this process, be sure you have a firm grasp on what's really been going on within your heart, and listen for God's direction so you can own the impact your choices have had on others, always within the framework of Jesus' grace.

Remember, the point isn't to beat yourself up emotionally, tempting though that might be. The point is to trust in God's promises of forgiveness and mercy for each of us, quietly listen and strive to grow toward Him, knowing *that's* what brings spiritual rest and healing. Jesus says, "I tell you, there is rejoicing in the presence of the angels of God over one sinner who repents" (Luke 15:10). Yes, it is healthy to own the pain and hurt we've caused others; we should feel broken up inside about it. But we must also remember God still loves us, and He wants to heal us, not see us lost in despair. God gets excited when you and I make decisions to repent, to turn away from something that has kept us bound and chained. Jesus shares many stories about how much God loves to see His kids turn things around and move toward Him again. Let yourself feel the remorse you should be feeling, but don't forget God is proud of you for finally choosing to do so.

Once you are in touch with the true impact of your actions on others, you are ready to begin allowing God to turn your heart away from those very things you are now aware of that make you ashamed. Paul does an excellent job describing this in 2 Corinthians 7:9-11. He had challenged the church in

Corinth in an earlier letter to repent, or turn from, some of the actions they were doing, condoning, and/or ignoring. The folks in that church did repent, and he describes the process for us:

I'm glad—not that you were upset, but that you were jarred into turning things around. You let the distress bring you to God, not drive you from him. The result was all gain, no loss. Distress that drives us to God does that. It turns us around. It gets us back in the way of salvation. We never regret that kind of pain. But those who let distress drive them away from God are full of regrets, end up on a deathbed of regrets. And now, isn't it wonderful all the ways in which this distress has goaded you closer to God? You're more alive, more concerned, more sensitive, more reverent, more human, more passionate, more responsible. Looked at from any angle, you've come out of this with purity of heart. And that is what I was hoping for in the first place when I wrote the letter.

What immediately stands out to me was the willingness of these people to listen to hard truths. They didn't make excuses; they didn't try to justify themselves. Or if they did, they acknowledged it and stopped doing so. They let the truths that Paul shared drive them to be more thoughtful and responsible for their actions toward others. Change is at the heart of true repentance. It's not that we somehow earn the ability to be forgiven by turning things around; that's a gift we can't give to ourselves no matter how hard we try. Only Jesus can give that gift to us from His blood shed on the cross. Yet because we understand how deep His forgiveness and love for us is, and how much He had to suffer to let us be free, we want to be different. We want our lives to honor God, and we are quick to own the ways our lives are in discord with His will, allowing Him to lead us to a path of harmony again. Not perfectly, but consistently.

As Paul makes clear, the whole point of repentance is to create purity of heart. It can be painful, yes. It can be very hard. Yet it is the very thing that makes you feel alive, that returns your passion for living, and guides you to embrace your humanity again, and all that entails. God does special things within each of us as we begin to embrace true, biblical repentance. As God changes our hearts, that change becomes a source of celebration not only to us, but also to those around us.

Another lesson from this passage is the willingness of the people in Corinth to allow outside help. They knew things weren't going great. I am sure several of them had spent time discussing, thinking and praying about possible solutions. I'm sure many others didn't really understand what the problem was, but they sensed the tension nevertheless. We are much the same! We get that there are issues. We may have even taken some serious stabs at tackling them, but we are in desperate need of outside perspective.

For some, pulling in your Wise Advisors will be enough. They will be your sounding board, and oftentimes give you sorely needed direction in how to begin mending fences. For others, you will *need* professional help. In fact, the more negative the impact of your actions on others, the more important it becomes to include professional support groups and/or counselors in your journey. Having people around you who deeply understand the nature of addiction, abuse, and other issues is crucial because they will understand your drivers and triggers in a way few others could. They will help you get in touch with your challenges and work through them far more quickly and thoroughly than if you go it alone. Let God use these people to bring about healing and reconciliation in your life.

Reconciliation is, in fact, another lesson from Paul's passage on true repentance. He mentions not allowing sorrow to leave us dying on a deathbed of regrets. Ouch! I've been there and done that, tossing and turning in my bed at night, reliving all the times I wished I'd done differently. I bet you have, too. Many times, those regrets stem from our actions with others. We regret what we did or didn't say, try or do. Jesus' goal isn't just to connect us back to God, but also to each other. We are told in Colossians 1:19-20, "God was pleased that all His fullness should forever dwell in the Son who, as predetermined by God, bled peace into the world by His death on the cross as God's means of reconciling to Himself the whole creation—all things in heaven and all things on earth." Reconciling our relationships to a place of harmony and understanding is part of why Jesus came in the first place.

Which leads us to the most visible expression of repentance—changed actions. When you love and care about others, and you've done the work you needed to do on the inside, it will show up in your behavior. Not perfectly, but consistently. The church in Corinth "turned things around." We all know actions speak louder than words, which is why we hear God telling us to repent in quietness. Your words, though important, aren't the things that will change your relationships. Changed actions will. We've talked a lot about what it means to apply changes to ourselves. Now let's look at how to apply it to others.

STEP ONE: OWN YOUR MISTAKES

You need to take the time to succinctly give a heart-felt apology to the ones you have hurt if it's appropriate to do so (see #3). An apology should never be given unless it is sincere. Don't try to justify. Don't make excuses. Remember Proverbs 10:19: "When words are many, sin is not absent, but he who holds his tongue is wise." Be wise by saying what needs to be said, and then nothing more.

When you do this, you may find the response you receive is an immediate, heartfelt reconnection and sense of happiness on the other person's part. Just knowing you are aware of your challenges and are actively working on them has the ability for some to restore their faith for and vision in you. If this is their response, and *they invite you to do so*, share your action plan. Invite them into your journey and include them as much as they are willing to be included. If they are willing to walk hand-in-hand with you by your side, consider that person a Wise Advisor, and include them in your process.

Oftentimes, though, especially when the hurt runs deep, this happy response will *not* be likely. When we've hurt others, they need to process that hurt, sometimes verbally. Women especially may feel the need to rehash their pain and emotion to let it go. Let them. It will be hard, yes. You will feel tempted to want to justify yourself, or for many men, you may to try to fix the problem instead of just listening and empathizing. Yet by consistently acknowledging the hurt you've caused, owning it without excuse, you give that person the best chance to forgive you over time and let it go.

Keep in mind that some people may want to know why you've done what you've done, and not in a rhetorical sense. They actually want to understand your drivers, what you are beginning to realize lies behind your actions. In knowing, they can understand and even offer empathy in return. Again, let them do the talking. Don't assume they will find this information helpful just because you think it might be. Ask them if they would like to hear what you are learning because you think it might offer them some clarity and emotional relief. They may want to hear; they may not. Your job is to be honest, humble, and offer any emotional support they need to be able to connect with you again in a healing way.

For others, it will require deep, profound and consistent change on your part before they will even be willing to talk with you. If they need space, give them space. If they need time, give them time. If they need several months of seeing positive change, give it to them. Wherever they land, honor their decision by respectfully giving them what they've requested. In doing so, you will slowly rebuild their trust.

I realize there are times when the other person needs to repent as well but hasn't done so. Remember: The only person you have control over is you. You can't apologize and repent as a ploy to make someone else apologize and repent. All you can do is focus on yourself. The other person is in God's hands. He loves them and cares about them even more than you do. Yet your positive decisions give the other person the best chance to change because you are not only making change real for them, but safe as well. Again, this shouldn't be your motivator because there is no guarantee. We change to become more like Christ. Still, it is important to remember that over time, even if it never shows on the surface, your actions do make an impact.

STEP TWO: LET YOUR ACTIONS DO THE TALKING

Speaking of actions, I've learned first-hand that it's the actions you change that will make the greatest difference in a relationship. As a young Christian, what began to change my relationships was not my words, but what I did. Choosing to do chores around the house without being asked, something I would normally pitch a fit over, made my mother stop and take notice of what I was doing far more effectively than any wordy pronouncement on the virtues of Christianity. Making a choice to be gracious and kind to my sister, regardless of how she treated me, went miles in healing our fractured relationship. Being as honest as I knew how when I made mistakes or wrong choices stood out in stark contrast from the finagling and lying I used to be known for. Slowly, over time, I began to rebuild trust and depth back into the relationships all around me. Keep in mind, not everyone changed *with* me, but even so, I felt a much deeper peace within simply from making those positive choices.

When people see you being more courteous, more patient, more giving, more (fill in the blank with what needs to be changed), it's hard to argue that you aren't different. As you grow in your consistency, other people's confidence in you will grow as well. Changed action walks together with trust. When we've hurt people, we've violated their trust in us. Trust takes time to be earned and restored. Aligning your actions to your words helps this process. Proverbs 14: 23 says, "All hard work brings a profit, but mere talk leads only to poverty." The hard work of growth and change brings emotional profit not only to you, but oftentimes to those around you, too.

The Apostle James talks a lot about faith/belief versus actions. He highlights the prophet Abraham, saying, "his faith and his actions were working together, and his faith was made complete by what he did" (James 2:22). When we make the decision to bravely, intentionally and consistently move toward God, it makes us complete. We move forward on a better path because it's God's path for us. Putting your money where your mouth is, so to speak, invites others to join you again on your journey. If you've apologized many times in the past with no real change, your actions become the *only* things that will truly win someone over.

In the gospels, Jesus originally called the apostle John one of the "sons of thunder." That can have some positive connotations, but I can also think of a few negative connotations that can go along with that title as well. By the time Jesus was done with John, he was known as "the one whom Jesus loved." To go from being known for your thunder to being known for your love—that's quite a transformation. It was the love Jesus showed John that transformed him, so much so that John later wrote: "We know what true love looks like because of Jesus. He gave His life for us" (1 John 3:16). Yet he immediately follows this by adding, "and He calls us to give our lives for our brothers and sisters."

Essentially, true love for God shows up in true love for others. True love shows itself by putting someone else's needs ahead of our own. Are you actively looking to meet the other person's God-given needs? Are you seeking to understand before being understood? Are you patiently looking to build others up for their own good? Doing so, once again, helps to restore relationship. As we are told in Ephesians 4:29, "Do not let any unwholesome talk come out of your mouths, but only what is helpful for *building others up* according to their needs, that it may benefit those who listen."

Sometimes what is best for you is not what is best for others. In other words, it's not always appropriate or helpful for you to talk or apologize to someone else for your actions, or to show them anything. Doing so would cause them more harm. When this is the case, and your Wise Advisor can be an invaluable resource in helping make that determination, your repentance may show itself by silently asking for forgiveness, or writing a letter to get your heart out, and then burning the letter, or even by making a sincere commitment before God to be different in the future. By prayerfully seeking discernment, God will guide you through this process. By putting the other person's needs before your own need to relieve yourself of guilt or whatever burden you feel you've been carrying, you are showing a heart that does love others and is repentant.

Never forget that people have the right to put up boundaries with us, to exclude us to varying degrees from their hearts and lives. Sometimes, we have to exercise that same right by loving someone enough to stand up to them, and not allow their negative behavior to shipwreck our lives. We set a boundary to be a wake-up call in their lives, always remembering they have the choice to wake up—or not. Our job is to set and honor that boundary.

When someone puts a boundary in place with you, honor it, even if it's hard. You may feel you've changed, and that the person should give you a chance. Remember: God always forgives when we repent, but the consequences of our sin remain. If someone is open to working through things with you, count yourself as blessed. If not, you must let them go into God's hands. In doing so, you are expressing an unselfish love that truly wishes for them what is best, even if it excludes you. You are deciding to honor their needs before your own.

STEP FOUR: SURRENDER

Ultimately, everything we do comes down to letting go of fear to embrace God's love, and to trust in Him. There are no guaranteed outcomes, no quick and easy fixes. But with intentionality and consistency, sprinkled with a good dose of grace, God can perform miracles.

Author Sonia Ricotti says, "Surrender to what is. Let go of what was. Have faith in what will be." Paul put it another way:

I'm not saying that I have this all together, that I have it made. But I am well on my way, reaching out for Christ, who has so wondrously reached out for me. Friends, don't get me wrong: By no means do I count myself an expert in all of this, but I've got my eye on the goal, where God is beckoning us onward—to Jesus. I'm off and running, and I'm not turning back (Philippians 2:12-14).

Pray for miracles, but trust God to protect you emotionally even if they don't happen. There's no point in trying to "win" people over to your side. Be true to who you are, and who you're being called to be. The right people will come alongside. You may be surprised by who they end up being, or they may be the very people you were hoping for. Either way, they will clearly be the ones God wants with you for your journey—and for theirs. As I have learned the hard way, sometimes losing the very thing we think we most need opens us up to receive even better things in our lives.

Resist the temptation to run ahead and fix things your way. You'll only end up with another nasty bruise on your forehead from the wall you ran into yet again. Surrender the outcome to Christ. If the relationship is fixable, which only God knows for sure, He will fix it, sometimes despite our complete lack of faith. If it's broken beyond repair, God will remove it, even if we had no doubt it would remain. Our job is to keep lifting it up to place in His hands, doing what He has set before us to do, and then surrendering the outcome to His "good, pleasing and perfect will" (Romans 12:2).

One of the most intentional action steps you can take with your key relationships is to apply the principles you've learned—vision, connection, connection with others, bravery, intentionality, consistency, boldly shine—to the relationship itself. Take the time to re-create a God-given vision for where your relationship can go. Be sure it's God's vision for you, not your own vision masked as being God's.

That means your vision should be realistic. Too often, we create a vision for our relationships, especially our family relationships, loosely based on *Leave it to Beaver* and *The Brady Bunch* episodes. Man, have I been there! I got so attached to an ideal that the ideal itself became an idol in my life, something I unknowingly worshipped. I was more interested in maintaining an image instead of embracing what I actually had in front of me. I should have fought to engage with the people I loved in a real, tangible way, to embrace the messiness that comes with family life. But I clung to the illusion over the relationships.

When my vision was an idol, it made me question my decisions, and even struggle to enjoy the good moments because I was too busy worrying and analyzing about what was or wasn't, or constantly wondering if I was settling, or being too much of one thing or not enough of another. It was exhausting! How freeing it was when I allowed God to smash that idol for me, and replace it with a flesh and blood vision, one that was driven by Christ and not by my need for perfection. Everyone around me benefitted from that change.

You will know when your vision is being driven by you, and not by Jesus, by the results you see. Jesus says, "Make a tree good and its fruit will be good, or make a tree bad and its fruit will be bad, for a tree is recognized by its fruit" (Matthew 12:33). Put another way, if your vision comes from God, it will begin to materialize and you will experience positive change.

Here are some examples to consider:

MY VISION	*GODLY VISION*
I want my family to be the best on the block, and for my kids to be really popular.	I would like to see my family be connected and close, to support each other even when it's hard.
My spouse and I will wake up every day in each other's arms, joyful	My spouse and I will love and respect each other most days.

and full of love for each other at all times.	We will consistently make time for one other.
I will become the best parent around, and people will step back and take notice of my all of my effort.	I will intentionally work toward growing in my parenting skills, remembering to walk in God's grace for me, so my kids can benefit.
My relationships will be a great example for Christ, and motivate people to want to be more like us in order to experience Jesus.	My family will embrace our messiness and our challenges so we can become more like Christ, and be an example of hope and the power of what God can do, even through us.

Setting vision isn't about building yourself up, or reaching for perfection; it's about becoming more like Christ. Letting go of an unrealistic ideal frees you from operating from guilt or from consistent disappointment. There is no such thing as a perfect family, a perfect parent or creating a pain-free childhood for our children, no matter how much we wish it to be. We are not perfect. There was only one person who walked through this life perfectly: Jesus. We still killed Him. Perfection doesn't guarantee an outcome. Genuine, heart-felt, visionary change that is brave, intentional and consistent allows us to grow and produce good fruit in abundance.

With that in mind, connect with God so He can refine your vision, and connect with your Wise Advisors about your relationships, including professionals if need be. Bravely tackle the internal issues that need to be addressed. Do it with others if they are willing, but on your own if they are not. Remember, your changes do make an impact, and *your* change is all you can control.

Then make prayerful, thoughtful, intentional decisions and action plans about the relationship. Be sure to take it one step at a time, and make space to evaluate your growth and progress. Ask the other person if it's appropriate to do so, and if they are willing. Don't punish them if they don't give you the answer you were looking for. Seek input as well from your Wise Advisor(s). Since they are outside of the situation, they are going to give you unique advice and perspective, or help you know when you're on or off track.

Next, prayerfully focus in on growing in your consistency of action within the relationship. Keep your goals in front of you, pray about them often, and remember to walk in God's grace because you will make mistakes.

Finally, read the chapter on boldly shining and learn how to mark the important moments of growth in your life. Take the time necessary to acknowledge and be grateful for growth, even if it's only within yourself. Many times, however, it will be in the form of a healed, strengthened, transformed and boldly shining relationship that has grown and evolved into something strong and wonderful to behold.

This process is the same regardless of whom you are working through it with. If you need to repair a key friendship, use the principles we've discussed to guide you. If you need to set up boundaries to keep a relationship safe, and this can include spouses, ex-spouses, parents, siblings, bosses, and the like, use these principles to get your own heart in order so you can confidently honor what God is calling you to do within that boundary. And since it is a process, remember to consistently cycle through it for both your own personal growth, and to grow with others. It's each piece moving together that moves the wheel forward, allowing you to exit your tunnel with your heart intact.

CONCLUSION

Intentionality with others is a BIG topic. As we scratched the surface together, my hope is that you felt God doing some stirring in your heart about where you should go next. Just as you tackled being intentional with yourself, with God by your side you can also learn to be intentional with others. The key is to start the process.

SUMMARY

Repentance literally means "to turn," and signifies a turning point in your life. Repentance begins from a place of brokenness over what you've done, but it is placed firmly within the framework of God's healing love for you. It stems from understanding how much you've been forgiven, how priceless you are to God in the midst of your dysfunction, and allowing that love to motivate you forward. As you move forward, remember to give heart-felt apologies when appropriate, while keeping your focus on letting your actions speak louder than your words.

Use the process you have learned, including the next chapter on boldly shining, and apply it to any relationship that needs healing. Include the other person in the process if they're open to doing so. If not, commit to using the process anyway. Changes you alone make will still have a positive impact on the relationship.

FOR FURTHER THOUGHT

1. What is your big goal with the relationship you are focusing on? What should your action plan be?

2. What are some smaller, manageable steps to achieving this goal? What will your very first (or next) step be? How might you need to modify your plan as you move forward?

3. How can you involve your Wise Advisors in your process? How can you involve your significant other in the process if appropriate?

4. What are some ways you can be sure to let God drive this process?

CHAPTER 9

LEAVING THE TUNNEL BEHIND
Boldly Shine

"Arise, shine, for your light has broken through! The Eternal One's brilliance has dawned upon you." – Isaiah 60:1

God is in the business of transformation. It's what He does. The Bible is full of example after example of ordinary people living extraordinary lives. Within its pages we meet people who've gotten a new lease on life, men and women who made a decision to boldly shine for God, sometimes for the first time; sometimes once again.

Yes, the Bible also has examples of people who rejected transformation—people who stayed stuck, hopeless, bitter and full of anger. These were the people who rejected God and rejected change. These were the people who wanted God to come to them on their own terms. They wanted God to bow to them.

I'd like to tell you a story. I was a young 7-year-old girl, growing up in a beautiful home in the suburbs. School picture day was coming up. My mother sewed a lovely dress for me to wear. I was so proud of that dress because she made it just for me. The night before pictures, my mom put rollers in my hair so I would have pretty little curls in the morning. I was styled, primped and preened over, and I marched to school that morning feeling like a princess.

Here I am, with bouncing curls and a big smile:

The next year would bring big changes to our family. My mother and father fought a lot; it was a scary time. There were many nights I cried myself to sleep. Eventually, they separated and got divorced. My mom had started working a full-time job in order to provide for us kids. She did her very best, but she didn't have a lot of energy in those early days of learning to juggle a new career while taking care of three children.

When picture day rolled around that year, there were no dresses made; no preparations put together. In the midst of all the busyness, picture day was forgotten. I woke up and tried my best to look nice. I tried to do my hair, to look as special as I could. I didn't walk in that day feeling like a princess; instead I walked in feeling doubt and embarrassment.

When I got the picture back, I was ashamed. You can still see the marks where I tried to rip it up. My mom gently pried the picture out of my hands, gave me a big hug, and reassured me I still looked beautiful. She's the only reason the picture still exists.

Every year thereafter she made sure all my school pictures were special, but this one still serves as a reminder of the pain and confusion of that year in my childhood:

Life has a way of breaking us. It can knock us around, bloody us a bit. It takes something that was precious and special, and finds a way to try and destroy what we find most sacred. We look back and wonder where the inno-cence, the joy of the day-to-day went. We mourn what was lost.

Fortunately, my defeats are not the end of my story, nor do they have to be the end of yours. Eventually, I would hear God standing at the door of my heart, knocking and waiting patiently for me to let Him in. When I finally did, as David shares in Psalm 51, I let Him work on creating a pure heart within me. We've had ups and downs, God and I, times where I've trusted Him and times where I've fought what I didn't understand. I've had times of deep peace, hope and restoration, and times of deep doubt, hurt and confusion. Through it all, God has helped my faith to stay steadfast—which means ardent, dedicated, relentless, resolute, single-minded, true, unflinching, unwavering, constant, dependable, enduring, and faithful. Not perfectly. But consistently.

I told you at the beginning of our journey together that my biggest dream, bar none, was to have a marriage that would last forever, and that would honor God. On my wedding day, you can see my face is full of joy, of hopeful expectation:

But there's something else you could not have known. Let me tell you the truth of my story, the real ending of my tale. Before I married my husband, I had another ceremony. I married God. The Bible describes God's people as His bride, "beautifully dressed for her husband," (Ephesians 5, Revelations

21). So, I donned my wedding gown, veil and all. And I made vows with God in the middle of my dorm room. I promised Him that He would always come first, that I would love Him no matter what life would bring, and that I would remain faithful to Him until, at the end of my life, He brought me home.

You see, my biggest dream has come true. I am in a marriage relationship with my God, and we've been together for more than thirty years now. Like any great relationship, we've had our ups and downs, times where I've disappointed Him and let Him down; times where I haven't always understood Him, even though He's always perfectly understood me. But there's nothing I can't tell Him. There's nothing He wouldn't do for me if it's for my good. And His love for me has been unshakeable. Never once has He lost faith in me, even when I've lost faith in Him and in myself.

Nowadays, when I look at my smile I see that same girl from my second-grade year, the one that was filled with so much hope, the one who had belief in herself and what she could do. Only now I'm wiser, stronger, and infinitely more aware of how my strength and confidence come from God. He HAS renewed me and allowed me to once again boldly shine.

I look forward to hearing your story—because yes, you will have a story. You're writing it with God right now. Page by page, day by day, hour by hour, line by line. At the end of the day, God wants your life to be a love story—a story about how you worked together through incredible odds, you fought off enemies, you stayed faithful even though you stumbled sometimes. When at last you lay your pen down, it will be as a person who was victorious, who was transformed, renewed, and chose to boldly shine in this life just as you will shine in the next. That's my dream for you, because it's God's dream for you.

Jesus says, "You, beloved, are the light of the world. A city built on a hill-top cannot be hidden. Similarly, it would be silly to light a lamp and then hide it under a bowl. When someone lights a lamp, she puts it on a table or a desk or a chair, and the light illumines the entire house. You are like that illuminating light. Let your light shine everywhere you go, that you may illumine creation, so men and women everywhere may see your good actions, may see creation at its fullest, may see your devotion to Me, and may turn and praise your Father in heaven because of it" (Matt. 5:14-16).

God has big plans for your story, powerful lessons He wants to give you so you can then turn and give them to others in whatever fashion He shows you. It may be that you meet someone who is going through the same tunnel you've had to pass through. You can offer him or her compassion and encouragement for the journey. It could be the extra joy in your step that people notice. They may not be able to put their finger on why, but there's something different about you and they note it. God can use your experiences in a million different ways—and will—if you'll let Him.

Now let's go back to the very beginning. Remember, it all starts with a vision, with beginning to believe God has something greater in store for you than your present circumstances. We work to connect with God deeply during times of trial, fighting through whatever obstacles keep us from seeing His face because we know we're not strong enough to battle on our own—we need the King on our side. We remember to connect with others, to find those people who help empower us and move us forward on our journey. It requires bravery to keep fighting the battle, the day-to-day bravery that isn't perfect but doesn't quit. We make intentional life choices, both for ourselves and with others, so we can allow God's Spirit to work. Then we build on our consistency, learning to develop healthy habits that heal us. As we continually work through this process, we once again begin to boldly shine.

At its core, making a decision to boldly shine is about working from a position of faith. Within that choice lies a sense of peace, of hope, of confidence and trust. There is a renewed sense of purpose, of mission, and of joyful awe at who God is molding you to be. It's when you can step back and actually see and feel God's transformative work coming to fruition in your life. It's the life Paul describes in Philippians 2:15 that "Shine[s] like stars across the land."

So much about the transformation process starts by surrounding yourself with God's positive truths of who you are and what He wants for you. You have to take time to allow God to invest in you, and then step back and see what God has done; mark the moments of your victory and refine your vision as you listen for God's ongoing direction for your life.

Boldly shining is also about not accepting the "less" mindset. What is the less mindset? Being asked by society to be less. We apologize when we shine brighter than others. We are quick to put ourselves down when people compliment us. We let people shame us, bully us, and minimize who we are and what we're worth; oftentimes, we do it to ourselves.

Women have a tendency to balk at doing something special for themselves, concerned they're somehow being selfish, particularly if they have kids (after all, shouldn't the kids come first?). Men can stuff away all sorts of emotion because they fear being viewed as weak, as somehow being less of what a "true" man should be. All of us can struggle with trying to define ourselves by what we achieve, instead of letting our achievements reflect who God has made us to be in our core.

Being less doesn't honor God. Remember—He's given you your talents, your strengths and gifts. To make light of that is to make light of Him. To own them as belonging to you instead of gratefully acknowledging where they come from is to deny His presence. And to willfully push them aside is to miss the hand of God showing up in your life and powerfully authoring your love story.

Writer Holley Gerth puts it this way: "Telling [people] they're not allowed to receive is one the of subtlest and most dangerous tactics of the enemy. He might not be able to make us ineffective by falling into major sin but he can accomplish the same thing by driving us to become utterly empty and exhausted." God wants to fill you up and "satisfy your desires with good things so your youth is renewed like the eagle's" (Psalm 103:5). Let's unpack together those final pieces, the last little cogs, that get the wheels rolling completely forward toward a transformed, boldly shining life.

SURROUND YOURSELF WITH TRUTH

If you walk into my office or my home on any given day, you will see the normal paraphernalia laying around—family pictures, personal mementos and what not. But you will also pretty quickly notice something else: quotes, images and lists displayed in key places. Sometimes I have a scripture or two written on my bedroom mirror; sometimes they show up on my bathroom mirror. I always have a few verses and quotes within immediate eyesight near my office desk. My action list is always at my desk.

I have a vision board, something God and I prayerfully craft together each year that is a visual representation of what He's leading me toward. I have two very specially crafted scrolls, rolled up in such a way that only God and I know what's written in them, but they contain the life goals God has laid out for me. All around me, I constantly surround myself with God's spiritual truths for me.

When you're under attack, when you're feeling demoralized and empty, you need constant reminders of how precious, how important, how sacred you are to God, because let me tell you—everything else around you is going to try to tell you otherwise! In the midst of all the put downs, let downs, and hard to swallow realizations, knowing the greatest presence of all is in your corner is sometimes the only ray of light in what can feel like a very small, very dark tunnel.

There have been times where I've read one of my spiritual truths, and have broken down sobbing, holding onto that scrap of paper or my Bible like a true lifeline. It was the only positive, good thing I had in the midst of a lot of ugly. It was the only thing that kept me holding on. That's why it's so important to surround yourself with truth.

We've discussed creating simplified priorities and goals, of finding our spiritual truths and writing them down. These are the very things you should post all around you. Post them anywhere you need to in order to keep those ideas on your radar. I have even been known to place some favorite quotes or most salient goals on my car dashboard so that whenever I get in the car, I read it and remember. It doesn't need to be anything fancy or creative, unless creating them that way inspires you. Some of mine have been crafted with absolute care; some are written on torn scraps of paper. How you do it isn't nearly as important as actively placing these reminders of worth and intentionality all around you.

Remember, the truths you post should tie into what you wrestle with most or need consistent reminders of. If you always strive for perfection, your scriptures/quotes/images may focus on accepting that your best is enough. If you struggle with defining yourself by how others view you, your scriptures/quotes/images may be the important reminders that it's your own path you walk, not someone else's. You need to define yourself by God's view of you; you have nothing to prove to anyone else. If you're like me, they will probably be a combination of a few things.

Keeping your goals and action steps visible is equally important. How many times have you made a list you felt great about, only to misplace it and dig it out months or years later, never having completed a single item? The enemy will do everything he can to distract you. That's why posting them around you is so important. King David, a man who overcame intense life obstacles, understood this when he said, "I will meditate on Your precepts, and contemplate Your ways" (Psalm 119:15). Meditation and contemplation both imply spending lots of time going over something again and again until it becomes deeper, richer and more tangible in your life.

Inevitably, someone always asks me if surrounding myself with positive truths actually works. In other words, do I always look at them and somehow feel instantly refreshed and faithful. Uh … no. Of course not. Most days, they're just sort of there in the background, brief visual reminders that I'm not on this journey alone. Still, I have discovered that over time, keeping my spiritual truths and goals around me helps me to internalize them, to really begin to own them and make them mine. The scriptures, quotes, goals, lists and images around me also change and evolve as I change and evolve, and they reflect God's ongoing refinement of my life's vision.

Yes, there have also been times I've thrown that paper or my Bible down with disgust, mad and hurting; or, in frustration, threw my list in a drawer and slammed it shut. But in the end, I always come back and pick it up again, doing battle to stay centered with my Creator. So even though I've lost some individual battles, I grab hold of my bravery and allow God to remind me He will always win the overall war. And He has, time and time again.

Sometimes I've put images or words on my vision board that felt way out of reach for me in that moment. I only put them there because I knew God was asking me to, but on the inside, I felt complete skepticism. I have consistently been humbled to find that very concept materializing in my life within the next year or two. Remember: God is faithful even when we are faithless (2 Timothy 2:13).

So even if it feels silly to you, post a few spiritual truths around you in conspicuous places. We've already talked about focusing on "whatever is true, whatever is honorable and worthy of respect, whatever is right and confirmed by God's word, whatever is pure and wholesome, whatever is lovely and brings peace, whatever is admirable and of good repute; if there is any excellence, if there is anything worthy of praise, think continually on these things [center your mind on them, and implant them in your heart]" (Philippians 4:8). Keeping your spiritual truths and goals around you is an integral part of that process, and over time you will begin to appreciate their value.

ALLOW GOD TO INVEST IN YOU

Boldly shining is also about creating space to get energized doing the things that fill you. When you are in times of deep struggle, it's easy to let the things you enjoy slip to the wayside. You're in full-blown crisis mode, trying to stay afloat and prayerfully find solutions, the sooner the better. I realize the last thing on your mind is taking time for yourself.

Guess what? You still need to. It doesn't have to be a big production. It can be as simple as buying the cup of joe you like, and savoring it as you read over your favorite magazine. But making the time to allow God to invest in and build up your spirit is a priceless gift that will not only bless you, but everyone around you, because it allows you to feel more centered emotionally, if even for a moment. It gives you a sense of normal.

For some people, this is the hardest step in the boldly shine process for them. They love doing for others, but they have a hard time doing for themselves. They have a hard time receiving. Yet allowing God to invest in you is such a pivotal piece of God's restoration of your soul. As we've talked about previously, when we become believers, God places a piece of Himself within us to help guide us—the Holy Spirit. What you may not realize is that to God, that makes your body His temple. That's right. He views you as sacred space.

In 1 Corinthians 6:19 we are told, "You surely know that your body is a temple where the Holy Spirit lives. The Spirit is in you and is a gift from God. You are no longer your own." When you take time to do the things that fill you up inside, you are also fueling God's spirit within you.

The Apostle Paul tells us, "Do not quench the Spirit" (1 Thessalonians

5:19). When you deny yourself the things that bring you joy, you could be quenching the very Spirit of God. After all, who created you to love that hike in the woods? Or the feel of a nine iron in your hands? Or the smell of the flowers you're planting? Or the spray of the ocean in your face? Or that sense of being treasured and special when you're being pampered? God did!

For me, I'm an outdoors girl. There's something about being outside that restores my soul. Whenever I'm out in nature, I sense God's presence. It fills me with joy; it reminds me of God's enduring presence. I also feel that way about music. Sometimes I find just the right song that expresses things to God on my behalf in ways that my own words can't express. Listening to songs that inspire and uplift me fill me with a deep sense of determination and joy. We all have things we do that fill us just like that. Those are the things I'm talking about making time for.

Whenever you feel guilty for pulling away for a bit to allow God to nurture you, remind yourself that the stronger you feel emotionally, the better you are for everyone around you, and the more capable you will feel to tackle your challenges. I have found, in fact, that sometimes a solution I just couldn't seem to find will come to me after I've decided to completely take a break and focus on allowing God to fill my spirit. Suddenly that elusive answer is right there in front of me, like it's been waiting for me all along. That's the power that comes from allowing God to invest in you.

I realize that for some of you, the very tunnel you find yourself in is one that was created from your own selfishness. You may be the person who loves getting filled so much, you've done it at great expense to those around you. Let's talk about this briefly.

There are many drivers behind what motivates us to be selfish, but for me it often circles back to not trusting my needs are going to be met by God or others, so I forge ahead to meet them on my own. Another piece of what motivates me toward selfishness is an unwillingness to pay the cost. In other words, doing what I want to do is far easier than actually having to face up to a tough situation that requires selflessness and thoughtful reflection on my part. I get lazy or cowardly, neither of which are very attractive.

Knowing the drivers behind my selfishness allows me to check my spirit with God. It reminds me to keep what matters most in front of me—my walk with God, my family and friends, and then my career and everything else—instead of allowing myself to get swept up in my own agenda again, or opting for the easy route. When I know I'm honoring the most important priorities in my life, I can breathe much easier when I'm making the time to allow God to invest in me.

Even if you are intentionally tackling selfishness in your life, you will still need to make time to allow yourself to be refreshed. If you never allow your-self reasonable breaks, you will run out of steam. I have a friend who worked so hard at his career he literally jeopardized his health. He had to take a six-month sabbatical just to recover. When you don't stop, you become like a car the driver keeps driving long after he should have stopped for gas: eventually the car will shut down and movement won't be possible, usually at the most inconvenient time. Be wise, and include your wise advisors in your process, but you are still wired with a God-given need to take breaks to be refilled.

Yet I would also challenge you to rethink what it is you find energizing. Let's say you're working on a challenging issue in your marriage. You know it will be an uphill battle, one that will require intentionality and consistency on your part for some time to come. I promise you when you begin to experi-ence moments of breakthrough and connection, when you begin to see God showing up in your marriage, it will feel energizing. We're going to touch on marking those important moments next, but realize there is something divine and special you experience as God begins to transform your situation. It's very difficult to put into words because it's *that* amazing.

We are told in Galatians 6:9, "May we never tire of doing what is good and right before our Lord because in His season we shall bring in a great harvest if we can just persist." The harvest you will reap as your life changes isn't just a good one, but a great one. In time, you will begin to realize this will fill your spirit in very rich, tangible ways.

MARKING THE MOMENTS

Marking your moments of victory with God is an easy step to miss be-cause we tend to look for the last pages of our story instead of remembering that it is being written even as we speak. We each, you and I, have shining moments throughout our life, both big and small, and learning to celebrate and mark those moments is extraordinarily important. Marking moments, in fact, is part of how you become aware of God's presence working in your life.

God loves to celebrate! He likes to do things up right, to mark important moments in a way that lasts, often throughout generations. Let's briefly walk through some boldly shining moments in the Bible together—moments in which God did some powerful things in people's lives and marked them in a prominent way.

While you may be familiar with God parting the Red Sea, you may not be as familiar with the nation of Israel crossing the flooding Jordan River. God's leader Joshua tells us, "Now the Jordan is at flood stage all during the harvest. Yet as soon as the priests who carried the ark reached the Jordan, and their feet touched the water's edge, the water from upstream stopped. It piled in a heap a distance away" (Joshua 3:15). The priests stood on dry ground while the people crossed. This was big stuff.

To mark this victorious moment, "the Lord said to Joshua, 'Choose twelve men from among the people, one from each tribe, and tell them to take up twelve stones from the middle of the Jordan from right were the priests stood … and put them down at the place where you stay tonight … These rocks will always remind our people of what happened here today" (Joshua 4:2-7). God wanted them to mark the moment, to have something they could look to as a reminder of His faithfulness when times were tough.

In the Old Testament, there was a solid gold ark of the covenant that contained important reminders of God's victories, and His directions for the people's lives (yet another symbolic representation given by God). When the ark was being brought to the capital, the prophet Samuel tells us, "David and all Israel were celebrating with all their might before the Lord, with castanets, harps, lyres, timbrels, sistrums and cymbals," and that, "David was dancing before the Lord with all his might, while he and all Israel were bringing up the ark of the Lord with shouts and the sound of trumpets" (2 Samuel 6:5, 14-15). Clearly, they understood the importance of marking the moment.

There is ceremony after ceremony listed in the Bible. There are examples of people marking victorious moments in prayer, in dance, in song, and in the making of monuments. There are small celebrations and parties, and big ones including things like the Passover celebration in the Old Testament, and the Lord's Supper in the New Testament.

Jesus gives us some insight into why such things are important when He institutes the Lord's Supper (or communion). He says, "Take this [bread] and eat it. Do this to remember me," and, "this cup is the new covenant in my blood; do this, whenever you drink it, in remembrance of me" (1 Corinthians 11:24-25). Jesus knew we needed to be reminded of His great, eternal love for us; He knew how easy it would be for us to get caught up in life's storms and forget that He is ever faithful. He knew we would need something tangible to keep His victories for us in front of us.

God loves to celebrate your victories with you, big and small, and it honors Him when we take time to mark those moments. I have marked my God-given victories in many ways over my lifetime. Sometimes I celebrated in ways I felt God was prompting me to take. Sometimes my actions came from my own heartfelt desire to honor God. I have gone out to the wilderness and sung love songs to Him. I have written Him love letters of gratitude. I have taken things that were valuable and precious to me, and buried them somewhere that only God and I would know about, all to mark my love for

Him and His blessings in my life.

Like David, I have danced before the Lord. Unlike David, I felt uncomfortable and odd, but I did it anyway because I felt God nudging me to do so. Even marrying God back in my college dorm room was a way for me to mark an important moment in my life with Him, a way to always remember His guiding presence in my life. I had no idea at the time how profound that moment would later become.

The first month I met all my financial obligations on my own without child support, I made a special meal and celebrated with my children. They didn't know why I made the meal; that was between God and me. But it made my heart smile to do it for us.

When I bought my first house a few years after being single again (it was one of those items God nudged me to put on my vision board that made no sense to me at the time), I marked the moment by inviting my Wise Advisors and close, spiritual friends over to dedicate my home to God. We spent time praying and praising Him, asking for His blessing and to use the space for His good purposes.

I have celebrated in small ways, too. Sometimes it was a prayer time where all I did was thank God for His love for me, and for guiding my path even when I doubted and wavered. Other times it has been as simple as just sitting back, looking up, and acknowledging His presence in my life, taking a moment to share my gratitude with Him.

During particularly tough life seasons, I would thank God if I had an entire hour or two that were good, or if I managed to get through an entire day feeling fairly okay. When I started stringing a couple of those good days together, I had to really stop and acknowledge that victory, or when the next challenging day came, I would forget there had been anything good in between.

When life is that difficult, it is even more important to thank God for those little windows of victory. If not, you can quickly get bogged down in what didn't go right, losing sight of what did. Every moment your head is above water is a moment you are remembering to walk in His strength instead of your own. Thank Him; acknowledge it. Doing so reminds you that His hand will continue to reach down again and again until you are completely back on dry land. It keeps you from feeling hopeless.

As those victories grow, so will your confidence and faith in what God can do in your life. With each celebration, big and small, a little piece of spiritual armor is put into place to protect you against the enemy. This is part of how you "put on the full armor of God so you can take your stand against the devil's schemes" (Ephesians 6:11). Our expressions of faith become our shield, "extinguish[ing] all the flaming arrows of the evil one" (v. 16).

Those expressions can be as varied as God is. Sometimes I have been nudged to create tangible reminders of God's faithfulness to me. My scrolls and my vision board I talked about earlier are examples. I still have a stone from the very first planning retreat for The Dented Fender Ministry, the non-profit I created to help people who feel spiritually stuck. Some people create art, or write songs, or buy something tangible that becomes an emblem between them and God. These are powerful, visual reminders that can be pulled out during times of weakness and doubt to remind us God is on our side.

LINE IN THE SAND

I have also taken time to mark the moments I have drawn an important line in the sand with God. The Old Testament book Haggai gives us a great example of this. God had been opposing the nation of Israel to get them to look up and notice they were neglecting their number-one priority in life: their walk with God. God used Haggai to clearly bring this to their attention, and the people responded. We are told in Haggai 1:12, "the whole remnant of the people obeyed the voice of the Lord their God and the message of the prophet Haggai." In other words, they were willing to do what needed to be done, to start prioritizing their lives differently and from that point forward, to honor God.

Through Haggai, the Lord tells His people, "Now give careful thought to this from this day on—consider how things were before one stone was laid on another in the Lord's temple. When anyone came to a heap of twenty measures, there were only ten. When anyone went to a wine vat to draw fifty measures, there were only twenty" (Haggai 2:15-16). He then continues by saying, "Until now, the vine and the fig tree, the pomegranate and the olive tree have not borne fruit. 'From this day on I will bless you'" (2:19).

God was very carefully marking a moment with His people. There was a very definite line drawn in the sand, one that made clear that there was a before and an after. This type of moment marks a prominent turn in the road, a decision to repent or do something in your life decidedly different than the way you were doing it before. It could be a healthy boundary you are putting into place, or a long favored, negative pattern you're being called to leave behind.

When I became a Christian, it was a line I drew in the sand with God. It was a decision that said from this point forward, I would live my life differently. My choices would reflect that line in my life—not perfectly, but consistently. And I marked that moment. When I decided to quit doing drugs and sleeping around, my life reflected that change. I had setbacks; my steps weren't always forward. But I kept taking those steps because I knew the line had been drawn, and the moment had been marked with God.

When I was going through my tunnel, I had to draw some boundary lines. I had to decide with God how I would consistently handle certain people and situations in a way that would honor my faith. This was a process over time, and those lines were never arbitrary or made without deep intentionality. Yet, in listening to God's call to make them, my heart began to heal and my life began to experience incredible growth and transformation. That's the power behind marking important spiritual moments.

Know that lines in the sand should always be drawn with God behind you, and at His urging. I say this because there's nothing the enemy loves more than to follow behind you and erase those lines whenever he can, something we see over and over again with the people of Israel. They kept promising to change, but it wasn't lasting. We talked about this at length in Intentionality. That's why drawing a line should be an intentional decision, not something you've done lightly, or because you've decided you're fed up (even if you are). It should be done because you've cried out to God, and He has answered you and called you to draw that line, and to mark that before/after moment.

His answer doesn't necessarily have to take time to find. It can be done in a moment, accompanied by a deep sense of the rightness of what you're doing that allows that line to be etched before you. Just remember: we draw a line to honor God and His calling on our life, not to challenge ourselves or as a way to motivate ourselves on our own.

WRITE YOUR STORY

The beauty of marking your moments with God, big and small, is that it reminds you God cares, and it allows you to slow down enough to see the ways He is shaping your life. Then, when hard and challenging times come, or when someone tries to erase your line, you can take out those victorious moments and symbols as memories of God's faithfulness to you. When you're tempted to give way to fear, they remind you instead to lean into God's peace that passes understanding and trust that He knows what He's doing, even if it doesn't make sense in the moment. They become your medals of honor, your badges of courage, the jewels in your spiritual crown.

Remember, it's not the size of the victory that matters. What does matter is taking the time to acknowledge them, to cherish those moments in your heart, and allow them to become the strengthening tool God designed them to be.

It's in marking these moments, and taking the time to acknowledge God's presence in your life, that you continue to write your own love story with God. And as each page is turned and each chapter is finalized, you will step back and marvel at what has become an epic story about tragedy and triumph, about great victory snatched from the jaws of certain defeat. You will join the ranks of many great men and women who have gone before you, enduring hardship only to find peace and joy hidden right there in the middle of the storm.

Of them, Paul says, "And what more shall I say? I do not have time to tell about Gideon, Barak, Samson, Jephthah, David, Samuel and the prophets, who through faith conquered kingdoms, administered justice, and gained what was promised; who shut the mouths of lions, quenched the fury of the flames, and escaped the edge of the sword; whose weakness was turned to strength; and who became powerful in battle …" (Hebrews 11:32-34). YOU will become the hero in God's love story for your life. You will become a part of what God calls His "great cloud of witnesses" (Hebrews 12), who, through their own decision to boldly shine, encourage and empower others to reach for healing too.

"For I know the plans I have for you," declares the Lord. "Plans to prosper you and not to harm you. Plans to give you a hope and a future" (Jeremiah 29:11-12). Let this be a moment where you step back with God, mark that line in the sand, and move forward toward true transformation and healing. As you do, watch your life begin to boldly shine out into the world, reminding people that with God, it is never too late for any of us.

SUMMARY

We boldly shine when we approach life from a position of faith hand-in-hand with God. It's a decision to reject a "less" mindset and embrace God's spiritual truths for our lives. Part of how we do that is by surrounding ourselves with those very truths consistently, and to allow our vision to evolve and grow as we evolve and grow over time. We also allow God to invest in us, to build up our spirit, and to fill us so we can be strengthened for our journey. Finally, it also includes marking important spiritual moments in our lives, whether those moments are big or small. As we continually engage in this process, God adds to our faith, our peace, and ultimately transforms us to boldly shine.

FOR FURTHER THOUGHT

1.   What is one way you allow yourself to succumb to the "less" mindset in your life? How might you tackle it with God?

2.   What are some of your spiritual truths? Where are some places you can post them so you will be reminded of them daily?

3.   Think of at least one way you can allow God to invest in you, and make time to do that very thing this week.

4.   Take time to thank God this week for a victory He's granted you. Remember, it doesn't have to be big.

DRIVING WITH CARE
Being Intentional With Children

"Children are not a distraction from more important work. They are the most important work." — C.S. Lewis

Going through a dark, scary tunnel with kids in tow is deeply challenging. They may be in their own tunnel right next to yours, or they may be looking into your tunnel from the outside. Either way, kids are smart and they know about the tunnel you are in, even if they are very young.

Kids sense things in ways adults don't. They see through the lies we tell ourselves and we tell others. Even if they're very young, they pick up on the tension and mistrust, often by acting out themselves because they feed off the negative energy. They intuitively *know* when something isn't right with mom and/or dad, no matter how well you think you're hiding it.

None of us ever want to see our kids hurting. There are deeper places of pain you go to as a parent when you see your kids hurting. There were many, many nights where I begged God to take the pain away from my kids and put it on me. Yet the situation didn't change. They had to go through their own tunnels. But like me, they came through stronger for the process, which is a testimony to God. We have actually grown much closer as a family, even though we were close to begin with. I'm proud of them, and of where each of them has landed. I will share with you the lessons I've learned from our process together, lessons that come from the unique perspective of owning the title of parent. Think of this as my action plan, the intentional decisions I applied to my family. The great thing about this action plan, though, is that it is universal in nature and will help you apply your bravery and consistency to your family life.

As with any challenge, the first thing I would encourage you to do is take the time to go through the steps you've learned with your family in mind. Take the time to establish a God-given vision for what your family can be. This is especially important if family dynamics have changed due to divorce or the loss of a parent. Kids need a sense of belonging, which is why creating an identity for your family is so important. Let this vision guide your process, remembering to modify it with God as you move forward.

Connect with God consistently about your kids. He is the only one on this planet who loves them more than you do. Well, grandma may be up there, too, but you get what I'm saying. When you're walking others through challenge, especially your kids, you really need God's guidance. Too many times to count, I have experienced Him showing up in the midst of my heart-felt prayer to give me an amazing answer that had immediate impact on my kids. Take time to listen to Him. And don't forget to bounce your thoughts and ideas off your Wise Advisor(s). If you don't have someone in your life that is a successful parent you can learn from or emulate, make finding that person a number-one priority. Bible scriptures and books that center on godly parenting are great Wise Advisors, too. You *will* need help. Make time to find it.

Bravely take a good, hard look at the dynamics within your family life. If you're coming from a place of dysfunction (alcoholism, verbal, physical or mental abuse, depression, etc.), remember those things didn't happen in a void. They left scars and marks on everyone involved, and in ways you won't be aware of initially. Don't be afraid to really dig in because it's your best chance of not only helping yourself heal, but helping your children heal as well. Be careful when you start digging into your heart to do so on your own initially, or with just your spouse/significant other. Don't pull the kids into the process yet, other than to share that there is a process you're working through because you are aware of your actions. They need you to be the parent (which we'll talk about more) during this process, the one who has the map that leads to a safer, better place. It's not that you won't ask for input on the map, or for forgiveness for having lost the map for a time, or even for some of the directions, but you need to have some sort of map in place first before you ask.

Intentionally create a plan of action for your family. What is your big goal? What are some smaller, manageable steps to achieving this goal? What will your very first (or next) step be? How might you need to modify your plan as you move forward? What learning may you need to do, or new skills you may need to acquire to parent more effectively? You will need to very intentionally keep your finger on the pulse of your family, so you can refine your vision and goals as necessary.

As you begin to make progress together, working toward developing and maintaining healthy habits as a family, take time to mark the moments (see the BOLDLY SHINE chapter). Sometimes you will mark the moments alone, just you and God. If your son or daughter finally opens up to you about something, that's a great moment to do a happy dance before God. Doing the happy dance in front of your son or daughter? Not if you ever want to hear anything from him or her again! Now if that same child manages to get his or her grades back up to par, by all means celebrate together. Remember to use wisdom as to whether moments should be marked individually by you, or collectively, but mark them nevertheless, so God can build your faith up and strengthen your family vision.

Intentionally developing and maintaining healthy habits is really at the core of what it means to create a strong family. Think of each of the principles we've discussed as being a spoke in the wheel, with God at the very center holding each of the spokes in place. The entire wheel continues to move forward because, as a parent, you are intentionally maintaining the health of that wheel, prayerfully developing ways to keep it sound. Since God is God, He can keep the wheel moving when a spoke or two breaks down, but He is also amazing at fixing a flat. So regardless of where your family is at, God can get the wheel moving forward through your tunnel(s) again if you let Him. Here are some basic action steps to keep in mind.

BE THE PARENT

When you are hurt and you're struggling, you are in a needy, vulnerable position. Ideally, need will drive you to God and to stronger relationships. But if you let need take over, it can also drive you to ill-advised or unhealthy relationships in a desperate attempt to feel better. This is equally true with your kids.

When it comes to parenting, your child needs you to be just that—the parent. They don't need to become your confidant, your little mother or father, your emotional support or care provider, or be put in any role you thrust them into to make *yourself* feel better. It's not fair to them, and it's not even fair to you. It will stunt the growth of both of you.

I'm not saying kids don't need to help around the house, help pull their weight, and make valuable contributions to your family team. We'll discuss the importance of those things. What I am saying is that your kids aren't the place you turn to when you need solace. They should never be made to take the place of the emotional support a spouse gives in your life. There are so many ways that can backfire and end up deeply wounding your child, placing them in a tunnel you've created, or leaving them more lost in the tunnel they're already in. It also leaves you stuck because it keeps you from finding healthy ways to move forward.

I have seen a faulty view of what parenting is play out in many ways. Here a but a few:
  • Unhappy parents who try to live vicariously through their children

instead of working through their own tunnel to find happiness (helicopter parents). This kind of hyper-involvement doesn't let the child develop any sense of independence.

• Sick parents who expect their children to drop everything to take care of them, thrusting them into a complete caregiver role as if they are already adults. This robs them of their childhood.

• Parents who ask their children to be their counselors, going to them for all sorts of advice that a child shouldn't be asked to give.

• BFF parents who try to be their child's best friend and buddy in the way only a peer should be. This includes dressing like your teenaged daughter or son versus figuring out what looks trendy and hip but is still parent appropriate (something they will usually welcome helping with).

• Parents who assume their teenaged child is an adult now, ready to take care of themselves, so they completely take their hands off the steering wheel (no one needs you to be more present than your teenager—I promise!).

• Negligent parents who think kids are adaptable, so they will get over "it," whatever that "it" happens to be. This parent has a tendency to never take their child into consideration when it comes to decision-making. "Ah, they'll get over it. They're kids," is usually the excuse. Or, they emotionally let go of their kids all together, figuring the other parent can do the job.

• A steamroller parent who holds such a tight grip on the family reigns they smother the growth of their children, causing them to push away hard to find growth, or to get smothered and become ineffectual in the process. This parent takes the admonition to "be the parent" to the extreme. For them, it's all about control, about making kids bend to the parent's will.

• The Disney Dad or Mom syndrome. This is incredibly common, and stems from the guilt a parent feels when they are the one(s) who placed the child in a tunnel through their decisions. Divorce, adultery and abuse in any form are examples of this. The Disney parent then tries to bribe their children into liking them or tries to somehow make up for their actions by buying their kid(s) lots stuff or taking them to Disneyland. They try to "buy" their way back into their child's heart.

• The enabling parent who feels so bad about what their children are going through, they try to make up for it by being overly permissive or making excuses for their child's bad behavior. They always have an excuse for why the bad behavior is okay or needs to be tolerated.

What your children most need from you during times of crisis is to still be the parent. They need you to show, through your example, how to move through a tunnel. Your children will have to go through some tough tunnels in life. Your job as parent is to show them how—with God—they can navigate through each tunnel successfully. If they are in a tunnel themselves, your job is to lead and teach through example as you navigate through your own.

You are the most important Wise Advisor in your child's life. You are there to listen and direct, not personalize their every move as a reflection of you. You are there to give advice, affection and love, but also discipline and consequences. They need to see your human side and your weaknesses, but also how you work through those weaknesses with God, as you strive to grow with Him in a balanced way. They need you to help them do the same. Don't abdicate your responsibilities. Your child needs *you*.

KEEP BOUNDARIES IN PLACE

In the real world, there are consequences for our actions, both good and bad. If you don't work hard, you're fired. If you do a great job, you get promoted. If you're kind to others, that kindness is usually returned. If you steal, you go to jail. If you continue to steal and don't get caught, you live like a spider in a complex web of lies that will ultimately ensnare you and drag you down to ruin. Without important internal boundaries in place, we can easily lose our way. As adults, we (usually) "get" this. Kids are still learning. The first place children learn the idea of boundaries and consequences is from you. If there are no boundaries and consequences, there is no learning.

Kids are wired to need boundaries. They need to know there are limits, places it's not okay for them to go to. It's part of why they push and test their boundaries with you. It brings them security to consistently find that line in place, even if they're showing the exact opposite reaction on the outside. All of us can likely think back on a time when we were young that we secretly hoped our parents wouldn't let us have our way, or we wished they had checked us more strongly in a particular area. That's because we didn't quite know what we were doing, and we needed someone with more wisdom and insight to step in and guide us, even if we also resented them doing so.

Establishing boundaries requires you first to teach your child what your expectation is, and then to hold him to that expectation. If she consistently meets that expectation, it should be acknowledged. If she misses that expectation, it should be corrected. If she's trying to meet the expectation but she's struggling, then she will need additional teaching, support and direction to be successful. This is true whether your expectation is for your child to not throw a fit in the grocery store, or to be home by midnight on a Saturday night. Both of those situations will require teaching the importance of the boundary, the triggers that may tempt a child to want to break that boundary, how to be proactive about those triggers, and the rewards that come from meeting that expectation. For the small child, it may a piece of candy he gets to pick out at the checkout line as a reward for his good behavior (or perhaps doesn't get). For a teenager, it may be that she gets to maintain the privilege of going out with her friends on a Saturday night, or that she loses that privilege. Either way, the boundary needs to be taught, and the expectation needs to be in place.

Having healthy boundaries in place is so crucial because it gives a child a sense of stability in a very challenging time. It gives them predictability in the midst of a lot of unpredictability. Since kids crave stability in the midst of chaos (as we all do), you will find them pushing their boundaries more. This can drive you crazy if you don't realize it comes from a place of questioning. Your child pushes not because she is trying to make a bad situation worse, or because he is thoughtless and insensitive. It's because he needs to know most of what is in place in his life is still there. And as you enforce those boundaries, she begins to realize that while one aspect of her life has changed, most of what is there is still valid.

Boundaries I worked hard to maintain included curfews, bedtimes, consistency in our routines, treating each other respectfully (with a heavy emphasis on word choice), maintaining grades, not quitting in the middle of things, and a culture of honesty within our home. I especially held to my expectation that I be treated respectfully as the parent of the household.

As parents, we feel guilt when our kids have to go through a challenge, especially if we perceive it as being our fault. Don't make the mistake of letting your child do whatever he wants in an attempt to appease your conscience. Keep your expectations and his boundaries in place. Doing so will help your child feel safe, and to know that while some things have changed, not everything has. As we are taught in Proverbs, "train children up in the way they should go; when they grow old, they will not depart from it" (22:6). So keep training.

STICK TO YOUR ROUTINES & RHYTHMS

Routines and rhythms are important in any family, but especially so during times of trial. There are days and times where these important aspects of family life need to be put on hold, but it shouldn't be for too long. Giving children a foundation of consistent structure helps them navigate through their ever-changing worlds more effectively. Parenting expert Dr.

Laura Markham says, "Children, like the rest of us, handle change best if it is expected and occurs in the context of a familiar routine." When change is unexpected, routine is even more important. Part of how we help our kids to heal is by continuing to hold them to what is familiar.

If your household has been changed, either due to loss or divorce, continue on with your routines. Simple things like continuing to do chores and having family meals together need to be continued, or in some cases, firmly established. It's okay if the way you do it is a little different than Mom or Dad did/does. Reassure them that even though it may be different, it's still important. As you continue to build into those routines, you begin to re-establish a healthy rhythm in your child's life. That structure helps her move forward.

Even if your family structure hasn't changed, don't let go of your family routines when you're struggling. You may need more help. You may need to make life a little easier for yourself with quicker meals or cutting back slightly on the number of games you attend. I know I did. But you still need to keep yourself moving forward, not only for yourself, but for your child.

Remember, too, we establish routines first by teaching them. If you expect your child to take out the trash, you first show her how to do so. You don't just tell her what to do; you walk through the process step by step *with her*. Never assume your child knows what to do. I am always surprised at how much they truly don't know! And it's unfair to discipline them for something you haven't shown them how to do, or haven't explained. Once I've taught my daughter how to take out the trash and shown her very specifically what my expectation is when I say, "Take out the trash," then I can hold her accountable for that action. But not until then. Some jobs take more teaching than others. The younger a child is, or the more complex the steps involved, or the higher thinking required, the more "hands on" you will need to be when you're teaching a task or a skill. I think I'm still trying to learn things my mother tried to teach me.

Balance is the key. In all my research, both academic and practical, the parents who have the greatest chance of success in producing healthy, happy kids are the ones who strike a careful balance. They may lean toward a more authoritative or more permissive style of parenting, but they have strong routines and boundaries in place, and couple those with a healthy dose of love and acceptance. God talks about this when He says, "Do not exasperate your children; instead, bring them up in the training and instruction of the Lord" (Ephesians 6:4).

We get frustrated when someone expects us to do something perfectly we don't really understand how to do, or when we don't feel valued or listened to.

Kids are the same way. How they feel and think needs to be taken into account. It's okay to modify the plan if new information comes to light in those discussions that changes your perceptions (yet another reason to have those discussions). But the number-one source of frustration for both of you will come from not teaching and training thoroughly enough, but then somehow expecting them to do something perfectly. Teach, train, and then consistently (not perfectly) hold to the routine.

MAKE TIME

Strive to make the time to understand your child. It's really easy for a kid's needs to get lost in the darkness of a tunnel, anyone's tunnel. One of the best ways to keep providing light for them is by connecting with them consistently.

We are each unique. No two of us are alike. The same is true of our children. Understanding what motivates one and allows her to feel connected to you can be completely different from what builds into the other. When your kids are in their own tunnel, they need to feel that sense of connection with you, to know that they are not alone on their journey. If you're in a tunnel, they need to know they still matter, that who they are, and what is important to them, is still important to you. This is part of why it's so important to stay connected with God during this process. When you lack the strength to move, God has a way of lending you the extra that you need to be present for your kids.

Each of my kids has very different interests. With one, our connection oftentimes came through music. He loved to show me new songs that he liked, or share with me songs he thought I might like. Giving him the time to share those things with me helped us stay connected. For another child, it was about video games. He loved them, loved to play them, loved to talk about them, and read articles about what was new and next in the gaming world. Now, I'm horrible at playing video games, which kept me from having to play them much because my son quickly realized I wasn't very fun to play with. But I listened, I watched him play, I'd let him share with me the latest article or discuss the latest game plot and what he thought about it. In doing so, I showed him that he mattered, and that who he was had value to me. In truth, it doesn't really matter what they share with you. What does matter is that they share, and you make the time to continue to connect with them.

There was a time in my life where I had to deal with some chronic health issues. Connecting with my kids during this time consisted either of my reading to them or playing quietly with them, one at a time, on my bed together a few times throughout the day. It was hard for me to do, but I made a point of doing it anyway because my children's need for me didn't end when I got sick. I could've felt a lot of guilt over what I couldn't give them, and there were times when I did. But they knew they mattered enough for me to make time for them, even when it was hard, and I had to trust in that. Interestingly enough, my kids don't really remember me being sick that much. I attribute making time for them as the reason.

Bear in mind we are to love others above ourselves. Loving your kids above yourself may mean doing things you don't love when you don't feel like it in order to connect with your kids. If they love Christmas and you don't, still work to make Christmas special. If it's the first year without a spouse around, it's going to be different. That's okay. Still celebrate. If they love watching action films or chick flicks and you don't, watch a few with them. When you consistently make the time to do what they value, you will find your own joy grow as you watch your child's confidence grow in his value and his ability to heal.

GET REAL

Don't be afraid to be appropriately messy. If you cheated, own it. If you are hurting, acknowledge it. If you did something horribly wrong, admit it. Trust can't be re-established without honesty. Note, I added "appropriately," since we approach children differently based on their age and their understanding. How you "get real" with a toddler will be very different from how honest you are with your teenaged daughter. Nevertheless, they need your honesty. Proverbs 12:22 says, "The Lord detests lying lips, but he delights in people who are trustworthy." So do your kids.

One of the most powerful examples you can give your children is to own *your* mistakes, and to not make excuses. This is part of how they learn to be responsible for their own actions. If you bashed their other parent, you need to apologize. And it needs to be a heart-felt apology. That person is still their parent, and not respecting the relationship is not respecting your child. No excuses. If you've yelled, thrown things around, made a mean-spirited remark, didn't take the time to listen, or hurt your child in any way, even if unintentional, give a heart-felt apology. Let them see by your own actions that you're addressing the issue. This teaches them to turn around and do the same.

Kids know you're going through something, and if they're going through that something, too, they will find your honesty helpful in allowing them to be honest—but to a point. They don't need to hear a lot of gory details, or about how you're really struggling emotionally about what a jerk their father or mother is. Yet they do need to know what you regret, or when some days are hard for you, or when you need their patience, or an extra hug because you're hurting. The first approach—revealing too much—alienates a child; the second invites them in to understand.

This was probably the hardest area for me to learn. I am a firm believer in maintaining a healthy boundary between my kids and myself as their parent. What I had to learn was it could keep them at a distance and even hurt them if I didn't let them in on what my feelings were. If my kids never once saw me cry during what they knew to be a tremendously difficult tunnel, what am I modeling for them? That it's not okay to feel emotion during times of trial? What a horrible lesson.

What helped me was to realize I was modeling for them how to handle ugly life circumstances. By letting them see me as real, I gave them the gift of allowing them to be real with me, too. By allowing them to see my weakness, it freed them up to share with me their weaknesses. Again, age needs to be taken into consideration. Telling a toddler mommy is having a hard day and needs a hug is fine. Breaking down and sobbing in front of a toddler would petrify him. Letting your tears show on certain occasions with your teenager and allowing her to see your humanity, on the other hand, can be powerful in the right circumstance. You will make mistakes as you find the balance. That's also a great learning opportunity for your children—it takes practice and humility to get things right.

There are two scriptures I have found to be incredibly helpful. Proverbs 14:25 says, "A truthful witness saves lives, but a false witness is deceitful." The more genuine my example, the more I am saving my children. Pretending everything is fine when it's not is a weak witness to them, one that won't hold up and protect them. The other is 1 Peter 4:4: "Above all, love each other deeply, because love covers over a multitude of sins." Making sure my children feel loved and respected by me is my surest bet to staying connected to them, even beyond childhood. I will make mistakes. But by the grace of God, the love I consistently *show* my children is, at the end of the day, more powerful.

CHECK YOUR HEART

We all have a default mode we go to as parents, and it's usually a reaction to how *we* were parented. We either identify with or reject those childhood experiences as we approach parenting with our own kids. Let's look at this in action.

I grew up in the era of "be home before the street lights are on." As a result, I had hours upon countless hours of unsupervised time. Many, many things happened during those hours, some good, but some quite bad. Yet, I learned to be very independent and strong, so I tend to view it as a positive experience overall. My mom was always there to listen, but she rarely got involved. She didn't attend a lot of my games in school, or get to know my teachers very well. Even though I don't find this to be the most balanced approach, I have judged my experience to be positive overall. Since I identify with it, this tends to be my default mode as well.

Now *her* parents were the opposite. They went to everything she was involved in, but in a way that made my mom feel smothered. They were constantly involved with her teachers, often in a negative and accusatory fashion, which she found mortifying. She hated how involved they were. So, she rejected their approach, and took the exact opposite position. If she had identified with it, she would have had the tendency to take the same overbearing approach with me.

The secret to parenting through crisis is to take a brave, hard look at what our default mode is, and then to prayerfully reach for a more balanced approach. For me, that meant remembering to check my kid's grades more often, connect with their teachers in a positive way periodically, and make time to get to as many of their events as I could. I didn't pressure myself to be at *everything*, which would have been unrealistic in my situation, but I made a point of being present in their lives. I had to fight to keep going with our rhythms and routines because it was an area I naturally wanted to check out from emotionally.

What is your default mode? Do you tend to make your kids the center of your universe in an unhealthy way, where all your energy, attention and passion goes into them with nothing left over for yourself, your spouse, or anyone else? Or do you tend to go to neglect, or to places of deep guilt? Do you get angry and argumentative, or overly passive and appeasing? Ask God and your Wise Advisors for insight. Or you can get really brave and ask your kids. They know. Once you find your default, begin intentionally crafting a more balanced approach. Read books, read scriptures, look for advice from parents you admire and trust. Work toward intentional growth in your parenting skills.

DON'T OPERATE OUT OF GUILT AND FEAR

Don't be a martyr for your kids. A martyr is someone who dies for a cause, sacrificing all. Yes, you should fight with your very last breath for your child's heart and soul, but never at the expense of your own heart and soul. Then what will you have left to give? This is one of the unhealthiest attitudes you can instill in your children. You teach them to not value themselves and own their worth as an adult, or to feel guilt over receiving anything good because they don't feel they deserve good things. Worse, you teach them to be motivated from a place of constant, gnawing guilt instead of being motivated from a place of love.

I have seen this played out in many ways in both my life and in the lives of others. In my life, my guilt as a parent stemmed from an unrealistic vision I had created in my mind of what my family should be, loosely based on *Leave it to Beaver* and *The Brady Bunch*, as I mentioned before. This wasn't a God-given vision; it was *my* vision. This ideal became an idol in my life, something I unknowingly worshipped. Again, I was more interested in maintaining an image instead of embracing the messiness that comes with family life. It made me question my decisions, and even struggle to enjoy the good moments because I was too busy worrying and analyzing. Every infraction from my children seemed like a poor reflection on my parenting, as if somehow achieving perfection on my part would create perfect kids. It was an incredibly freeing experience when I allowed God to smash that idol for me.

Letting go of an unrealistic ideal frees you from operating from guilt. There is no such thing as a perfect family, a perfect parent and a pain-free childhood, no matter how much we wish it to be. There was only one person who walked through this life perfectly: Jesus. And last time I read my Bible, out of our ignorance we still managed to kill Him. Perfection doesn't guarantee an outcome. Genuine, heart-felt, visionary leadership of your children that is brave, intentional and consistent allows them to grow strong and healthy souls, and to become a delight to your soul as well (Proverbs 29:17).

Part of letting go of guilt includes not letting yourself be thrown under the bus. What does that mean? It could be covering up for your spouse's sin by pretending you don't know, or that somehow, it's your fault. You may think you're helping your child. You're not. Lying and saying a parent really cares if the parent has intentionally abandoned the child is another example. Letting lies that are told about you go unchecked is yet another. You are maintaining an illusion for them that will be shattered someday, and when it is, so will their trust in you.

I have learned to share with my kids what they ask about, or to correct *without judgment* what is said about me that is untrue. If they ask a question, I answer honestly without elaboration. If they ask for more detail, I give only one more piece, and so on. Whenever I have erred on giving too much information, my child has reacted negatively. Just give them what they are specifically asking for or about. Help them figure out how to work through what you've shared, certainly, but don't lie. Deceit is the tool of the enemy, which is why we're commanded to rid ourselves, "of all malice and all deceit, hypocrisy, envy and slander of every kind" (I Peter 2:1)—even if the slander is about you. Love your kids above yourself, but not at the cost of your self-worth. And remember, your honesty and integrity will shine brighter and speak louder than any other words they may be hearing.

EVALUATE THEIR ACTIONS

"Young people eventually reveal by their actions if their motives are on the up and up" (Proverbs 20:11). Kids are master manipulators. It's just a gift inherent to childhood. Back when I was a teacher, I taught students how to write persuasive essays. When I introduced the concept, I would say, "Think about a time you really wanted to get something out of your parents. I bet you knew exactly the right approach to get them to believe you, and to do what you wanted." Their faces would light up, and they would nod knowingly. Kids know how to work us. No matter how good you view your child as being, they will try to manipulate you.

Kids also lie. Again, they test their boundaries and push their limits. It's what they do. The Bible says, "Folly is bound into the heart of a child, but the rod of correction shall drive it far from him" (Proverbs 22:15). You are that rod of correction in their lives, and just like you would do with anyone else, you need to *look at their actions over their words*. If not, you will go from being a positive correcting force in their lives to being duped and defeated as a parent.

When my kids were young, their lies were so obvious it was almost cute. I could almost see the wheels in their minds turning, roaming through a very limited number of possibilities. I had to work to not smile in front of them. Still, I disciplined them because I knew when they got older, that behavior would be a lot less cute and significantly more sophisticated.

You will be outmaneuvered as a parent if you look to your child's words over his actions. I had a student once who lied routinely. One time in class, we talked about a historic place, and this child insisted she had been there. Since she lied so much, none of us in the classroom were inclined to believe her. She was very hurt by this and went home to complain to her mom and dad.

In talking with the parents, I quickly realized they were unknowingly contributing to the problem. Their entire focus was on having the class acknowledge their error, and to tell her they believed she had been there (because she had). A more effective approach would have been to tell her that while they felt sorry for her that no one chose to believe her, she needed to own her actions. If she hadn't been lying so often, people would have believed her right away. She could have had an opportunity to share some really neat information with the class. They could have used the situation to be the wake-up call she needed, reminding her that such hurtful consequences are the very reason they have been challenging her about lying.

This same child was a very convincing storyteller. She had a way of making you believe she was being honest. She had a sincere look that would win an Oscar. But after multiple situations, it became clear she was the common denominator. Clearly, she had some challenges to work through, but the parents continued to look at her words over her actions. I get it. We want to believe in our children, to assume the best of them. But we also need to be wise. Choosing to tell her that her actions were speaking louder than her words, and that it was her actions they were going to address, would have helped nip the negative behavior in the bud before it grew into something far more destructive.

Fast-forward to the teen years, and let me tell you, you can't afford not to have your game on. No matter how hard things are for you personally, you've got to be very aware of what's going on with your son or daughter. Your child will tell you she is perfectly fine, but she could be planning to commit suicide. Your son can say he's at the after-school study session, but he's really out smoking dope with his buddies. She can tell you the new items you keep finding are gifts from her friend or boyfriend, but she's actually shoplifting now on a regular basis. Your children can lie to you and tell you what you want to hear about their purity, but then wind up pregnant or suddenly learning what it means to be a father. I'm not being melodramatic. These are real-life experiences.

Take a hard look at what your child is doing. If you suspect they are doing drugs, or struggling with depression, or socially withdrawing, or being promiscuous, or doing anything that makes your parent "Spidey senses" tingle, they are probably doing what you fear. Kids, especially older kids, will act out more when they are going through tunnels, so it is especially important to be vigilant during this life season.

Proverbs 19:18 teaches us, "Discipline your children, for in that there is hope; do not be a willing party to their death." It is your job to pull your child out of the fire, no matter how much they protest. Know what signs to look for (Google anything on the computer and I promise you will find more information than you could ever want). Then, take action and get immediate help. If the issue is severe, do not hesitate to pull in professional help immediately. Your quick and swift action could literally save your child's life.

There is an African proverb that says, "It takes a village to raise a child." Truer words were never spoken. Parenting is a really big deal. It takes focus, time and attention in a way nothing else does. It will require everything you have, and many things you don't have. That is why we need community around us. No one person can do it all on her own, and this is even more true when you are going through a dark tunnel of your own.

If you live near family and your family is supportive, count yourself blessed. Allow your parent(s) to come in and help. Who cares if they don't make the meals quite the way you would, or if their version of clean doesn't match yours, or they let your child cry a little longer than you'd like? The point is, they can help you get the time you need to periodically build strength into yourself, your relationships, and your walk with God. You will come back a more prepared, more present parent from the process, even if the kids are bouncing off the walls from a treat-induced sugar high.

And yes, you may need to create boundaries with your parents. You are still the parent, so it's reasonable for you to expect your important rules to generally be enforced. But they're also Grandma and Grandpa, and they will have their own, special relationship with your children that is important. Be clear on the non-negotiables in your children's routines. It's okay to bend a bit on less important matters. Having their help is priceless.

If, like me, your parents aren't close by, or they aren't a positive force to have around your children consistently, start building your village. Savvy moms and dads know they don't have time to drive Jimmy to soccer while getting Susie to ballet and Melissa to karate. They reach out to other parents and create things like car pools, and baby-sitting swap nights, and play dates so the kids can be at someone else's house, thereby getting (or giving) a bit of a break. Network with other parents. Go to the PTA meetings, if only to develop friendships with other parents. Who knows? They may end up becoming a Wise Advisor and a great friend. At the very least, they may alternate Thursday night driving responsibilities with you. Utilize your resources.

If you're a single parent, this is even more important. If I'm out of town on business, there isn't another parent to fill in the gap. If my parents can't make it to where I live, I'm going to be stuck if I don't have a plan. I have a few amazing moms in my life that I know—if push comes to shove—will be happy to take my daughter for a few days. They know I would do the same for them. I make a point of including their daughters on outings and trips, too, so I'm not just taking, I'm also giving in return.

Also, be sure to include teachers and counselors in your village. My children's teachers were an invaluable resource when my family was going through our individual tunnels. They were able to provide me with insight on how my children were behaving in the classroom and let me know if things seemed "off" or different. Kids can behave in completely different ways when they're at school versus when they're at home, as I would learn, and you'll never know unless you ask.

All three of my kids went through counseling at some point. Our school district offered peer groups for children going through divorce, but they also had groups for kids who were feeling bullied, or had lost a parent. They sponsored a "Girls on the Run" program that helps promote positive body image for girls. My community also offered free counseling services to anyone who lived in our area. I utilized everything that was available and relevant. Even if your child's school or community doesn't have the same types of offerings, your school's counselor *will* be aware of what is out there nearby, and available to you, oftentimes for free. Call them and find out. Give your kids they support they need to be successful. Be intentional in this area.

SURRENDER

Never forget your child's tunnel is not your tunnel! Even if your tunnel is caused by the same event, you will each experience it differently. Take the time to understand how your child actually feels without presuming you automatically understand. You don't. Only God truly does. Teaching your children to go to their Maker as they work through their tunnel, and helping them to make brave, intentional, consistent decisions in their lives is a gift you *can* give.

That said, your child still has the choice whether or not to follow. And the older the child, the more this is true. You can make a 25-pound toddler take a time out. You can't *make* a 220-pound 17-year-old take a time out if he refuses to. This is without a doubt the hardest part of parenting. There are simply things that are beyond your control. I have seen parents who did an amazing job of parenting, and their kids continually struggled. I have seen parents who had very weak parenting skills whose kids were amazing. At the end of the day, your child, like you, still has to make her own choices, and live with the consequences of those choices.

Continue to make yourself available and present. Continue to model unconditional love, but don't remove their consequences from them. When my son was younger and I would tell him I loved him no matter what, he would sometimes mischievously ask me, "Mom, would you love me even if I committed murder?" I would always answer, "Yes, son. I would. I would turn you in to the authorities myself if you did that, but I would visit you in jail every week." I would smile, and he would giggle, but I was actually quite serious. And he knew it.

While each of my children went through some very challenging times as we all navigated through our tunnels, my middle son struggled much longer and in more obvious ways than the other two. His reaction to being thrust into a tunnel was to reject everything about our family. Suddenly, he couldn't remember anything from his childhood. He went from making honor roll every quarter to struggling to pass classes. He tried on personalities like a woman shopping for sunglasses. He shut all of us out emotionally and kept us at a distance.

What I remember most about this season is knowing exactly why he was doing what he was doing, but also realizing that he didn't know why yet, and that he wasn't ready to find the answers. During this time, I kept asking him a lot of questions, working hard to find ways to connect with him, to keep him talking, and to let him know that when the time finally came that he was ready to explore his feelings, I was there waiting. By doing so, I maintained our connection.

As for his grades, I tried everything you could imagine. I talked to counselors and teachers. I talked to psychologists. I had him talk to counselors (who knew a kid could sit in perfect silence for an hour?). I hit up my Wise Advisors for suggestions and advice. I prayed constantly for him. I tried forcing him to study, putting a system into place. I tried talking with him about his grades every week, discussing every assignment. In a moment of pure exasperation, I even drove him down to the worst part of town and pointed out the drug addicts and homeless people, asking him if this was really where he wanted his life to go. I prayed with him, share scriptures, yelled, cried, cajoled. You name it; I tried it.

Finally, we were approaching the end of his junior year of high school. I didn't want to spend the last year or so of our lives together fighting. I told my son that while I believed in him and his abilities, I was no longer going to ask him much about his grades. He had to make the choice to care enough about himself and the man he wanted to be to pursue excellence for his own benefit. I made it clear I still had great vision for him, but I also made it clear he had to make the choice to believe it.

When he wasn't allowed to play soccer—a game he loved—during his senior year in high school because of poor grades, I didn't intervene or plead with the coach. I let him fully experience the consequence of his actions, even though doing so was hard. When he had to go to a regional campus instead of the university he wanted to attend, I didn't make him feel bad, but I didn't feel sorry for him either. I talked through what his plan was with him, and reminded him once again that I believed in him and his abilities.

During this time, slowly but surely, my son started turning his life around. We argued less. We laughed a lot more. He started to remember the good things from his childhood again, and to regain a vision for what his life could be like. When he went to college, he didn't come out of the gate swinging, but neither did he fail. He joined the military, and started regaining a sense of pride and self-discipline. He met other people who were positive influences in his life, and their successful behaviors helped motivate his own.

Now, he is not only a strong student, but also a leader on his campus. He's organized a club, mentored students, and taken the time to heal and invest in his family relationships. And yes, I am very, very proud.

Sometimes with our children, there comes a point in time where we've done all we can do as a parent. For whatever reason, this is one of those life lessons your children have to learn on their own. At this point, all you can do is surrender them to God, continue to be present and available, and trust God to do the rest.

Our goal as parents is to guide our children during the short time they are with us so they are able to make the right choices and choose the best path *for them*. Ultimately, though, they do choose their own path, and that path may be negative. If your adult child feels lost to you right now, or you are in an estranged relationship, or if your child is lost in addiction or devoid of hope, give all you can give, but then you have to surrender him over to God. Remember, "with God all things are possible" (Mark 10:27). God can repair in ways we can't. Thinking it's all up to us or it happened all because of us will destroy us. Own whatever it is you need to own, but sometimes the best thing you can do is surrender it to the Lord.

We are told, "And over all these virtues put on love, which binds them all together in perfect unity. Let the peace of Christ rule in your hearts, since as members of one body you were called to peace. And be thankful" (Colossians 3:14-15). Do your best to make peace with where things are, looking for ways you *can* be thankful, and never give up your hope, your vision, and your belief in the power of prayer for your child to change.

SUMMARY

When being intentional with your kids, always remember that you are the parent. You can't abdicate that role. Children still need boundaries, even more so in the midst of upheaval and chaos, and it's your job to create and enforce boundaries and routines. Be appropriately real with your kids, but don't play the martyr role with them, either. As you create or maintain healthy routines and rhythms for your family, listen to their needs and model growth and healing for them. Evaluate their actions so you keep the real story of what is going on in front of you. Create a solid community around your family to help support and guide you collectively through your tunnels toward healing. At the end of the day, give your children over into God's hands because His hands are the most capable of all.

FOR FURTHER THOUGHT

1. What are two areas to consider that most stood out to you? Why?
2. What is one step you can start taking to connect with your child on a consistent basis? What will that look like? What do you see the two of you doing?
3. What is your default mode? Identify one resource this week you can use to approach your parenting with more balance and insight.

ACKNOWLEDGMENTS

This book has been a reluctant labor of love for me. Reluctant because it wasn't something I ever really wanted to do. God had to sit on me—hard—for me to finally embrace this project and work toward making it a reality. Yet it has been a labor of love from the moment I embraced God's calling for me. All along, He has put the right people in the right places at the right time to move me forward and bring this book and ministry to fruition. I would like to thank a few of them now.

To Erin Campbell, my heart-felt thanks for being an early mentor in my journey. To me, meeting you was the first confirmation of my calling, and I thank you for those initial nuggets of wisdom you so freely shared.

To Cathy Baker, my co-conspirator in bringing this ministry to life. God knew what He was doing when He crossed our paths. I am deeply grateful for you and couldn't have done this without you. I may have written the words, but your heart is splashed across the pages. And Lisa Freson – thank you for keeping us both sane! I know the two of us together can feel a bit like herding cats, but you have become such a capable shepherdess. Thank you for keeping us dreamers on track. You both are remarkable women and wonderful friends. It's a blessing to work with you both.

To the Dented Fender board and team: I am blessed to lead such an intelligent, fun, capable and godly group of people! I have learned so much from each of you and I'm excited for what we are building together! This moment couldn't have happened without you.

To the fabulous Miss Patty Lane, my dearest Wise Advisor and cherished friend. You have listened to the tears, the doubts, the joys, the blessings and every high and low of my life and this ministry. I am so grateful I get to do life with you! You were my first editor, my first team member, my first cheerleader and you are still my first go-to in so many ways. "Your love has given me great joy and encouragement, because you, sister, have refreshed the hearts of the saints" (Philemon 1:7). I love you, Girl! It is an honor to be called your friend.

To Pete Bronson, my editor: I couldn't have asked for a better person to walk alongside me for this part of the journey. You are candid but thoughtful; you push but never too hard. Your thoughts and comments have made this a stronger book than it would have been otherwise. I have so appreciated having another wordsmith in my life who not only understands how someone can obsess over a single word but embraces that process. My heart-felt thanks for the crucial role you've played in bringing this book to life.

To Robert Lightner and the whole crew at Potter's Ranch in Union, Kentucky, where more than half of this book was initially written. Your gracious support that allowed me to get away to such a gorgeous space in order to write was such a priceless gift. Potter's Ranch has been a blessing to so many, and I'm proud to be a tiny part of its story.

To my Aunt Sue, my Wise Advisor extraordinaire: Your home spun wisdom and calm, loving spirit have been such a strong influence in my life. I always know you are there for me, and we will likely giggle about our graveyard experiences even in heaven. I love you so much! Thank you for being the sister/mother/friend/aunt/safe place that you are.

To Jo Anne Lyons for your wise counsel, Beth Guckenberger for being that sounding board I sometimes need, Tim Beatty and Randy Wilhelm for connecting me to people who became so crucial to my journey, to Lynn Maloney and Karen Wilke for all of your help early on.

Finally, thank you to my heavenly Father. I couldn't, wouldn't want to do life without You. Your loving care, Your powerful work in my life have been too profound to put into words, though I have humbly attempted in this book. My hands are open, Papa. All I am is Yours and my life is in Your hands. Thank you for pushing me toward this, and for your loving patience during those early stages when I fought with you about it. There's nothing in this book I didn't write without praying for and sensing Your presence by my side. May it achieve Your good purposes. I love you.

ABOUT THE AUTHOR

Barbara Lownsbury is a speaker, author, entrepreneur and single mother of three. She serves as executive director for The Dented Fender Ministry and currently resides in Cincinnati, Ohio. She has bachelor's degrees in history and elementary education, and a master's degree in education.

Barbara travels and speaks regularly at conferences, retreats and church services. Her reputation as a speaker and teacher is built on her ability to connect with people in a way that is relatable and genuine. She draws on her vast life and ministry experiences to pull in audiences with her storytelling, depth and humor, while equipping them with concrete tools to move forward long after they've gone home. This is her first book.

To request Barbara as a speaker for your next event or to learn more, please visit her website at www.thedentedfender.com.

Made in the USA
Columbia, SC
11 May 2019